IGNITING INSPIRATION

[A PERSUASION MANUAL FOR VISIONARIES]

Cover design and interior layout:

Evenson Design Group

www.evensondesign.com

to order additional copies, please visit:

For more info on Transformational Design®

Or John Marshall Roberts

Please Visit:

www.jmarshallroberts.com

or

www.ignitinginspiration.com

To Dad, for listening.

TABLE OF CONTENTS

Part II: THE DIFFERENCES: How do people differ meaningfully?

PART III: THE PRACTICE: Applying Transformational Design™

PREFACE

"If the doors of perception were cleansed, everything would appear to man as it is, infinite." - William Blake

Inspiration is what happens when we experience the truth behind the mind. Inspirational communicators are serving a function that our species sorely needs; they are putting us back in touch with our limitless creative potential, and reminding us that we are each authors of our own experience. This isn't rocket science—it's simple. But within this simplicity lies the hidden fate of our species and the sustainability of life on this planet.

The climate crisis, war, terrorism, racism, genocide, and drought—these are not problems, these are symptoms. The cause is hidden. We've designed it that way with a devious cleverness usually reserved for storybook villains. The true cause of our suffering is buried in our faulty notions about what it means to be human, and in our stubborn unwillingness to finally admit the timeless truth of who we are. Inspiration is our remembrance of that simple, joyful truth.

Who is this book for?

This book is for socially conscious marketers, business leaders, and activists who believe that communication should serve life and not the other way around. This book is for people who despise manipulation, cherish authenticity, and who cringe at the notion that they must sacrifice their conscience in order to make a living. Ultimately, this book is for people who care so deeply about the world we live in that they're willing to reexamine everything they think they know in order to make it work.

Here is my promise: If you allow yourself to truly absorb and apply the information in this book you will become a veritable wellspring of inspiration. Why? Because you'll attain unprecedented insight into the hidden dynamics of human inspiration, and you'll grasp very clearly how to ignite this feeling in those you meet—whether one-on-one, in front of bustling auditoriums, or through broad mass-marketing initiatives.

Please understand: the ability to inspire others is not a gift reserved only for masters such as Gandhi, Martin Luther King, and Barack Obama. Inspiration is an art, and it can be learned by anyone with the discipline to learn and an authentic intention to be of service. The simple fact is that inspirational communicators are masters at using symbols (words, pictures, sounds, etc.) to create inspiring new mental contexts from which people can act and live. In order to be a master at creating new mental contexts, one must first have a well designed *meta-context* from which to operate—a context for creating new contexts. This book is a surprisingly simple communication meta-context training manual based on real world research, and built for real world application.

Why should you believe me?

Someone once said that, in life, belief is the booby prize. This is true, because belief is always based on the mind, and the mind is forever in the past. If you want to inspire, you must be willing to enter the "fierce urgency of now" and trust your own instincts more than your beliefs. You must be willing to start listening to life the way a gifted composer listens to music, with an empty, expectant sense that something grand is taking shape right before you. No amount of belief will prepare you for this type of experience—only a *willingness* to put clingy beliefs aside in lieu of something more vibrant and compelling.

Having said this, let me indulge your critical mind for a moment by informing you that I am, in fact, uniquely qualified to be your guide. I have spent the last two decades developing, applying, and refining the ideas in this book. As a consultant I've used these ideas to help a variety of socially conscious clients—utility providers, museum start-ups, and design companies—to better understand and inspire their customers. As a professional speaker and media personality, I've used them to inspire thousands of people to access deeper levels of their own potential. As a musician, I've even used these ideas to write and perform music that has inspired thousands of people around the country and around the world.

Truth is, my entire life has mysteriously conspired to prepare me to write this particular book, at this particular moment in time.

So yes, I am qualified. But for heaven's sake don't believe me! Just stay silent and listen to that still voice behind your mind that always knows the hidden truth about everything. Take a breath and ask yourself: *Is this guy telling the truth? Am I inspired?* If so, keep reading. If not, move on. It's just that simple.

Think globally, drink heavily

Be forewarned: this book is not for the fluffy-minded or faint of heart. Although necessarily abstract and philosophical at times, this book is actually a down-and-dirty design manual for those who wish to roll up their sleeves and make a difference on a massive scale by turning the traditional tools of communication on their heads (and have fun doing it). To accomplish our lofty learning agenda we will start at the very core of the human being and build systematically outward toward the realm of the senses. When we're finished, you will never look at people, or the process of communication the same way again.

Our first task will be to clearly define the real problems with traditional initiatives so that we can tackle these problems head-on. Then we'll be ready to outline a fundamentally different approach to crafting communications called Transformational Design®. As you'll see, this is more than just a new communication framework—it's also an inspired new way of understanding what it means to be human.

Let's get started then, shall we?

Introduction

·····

An Updated Map of Human Nature

·····

The secret of success in life is sincerity. If you can fake that, you've got it made." – Groucho Marx

Remember that old story about Christopher Columbus trying to sail around a world that was—according to the maps of his day—totally flat? That's what is happening today. The vast majority of communication professionals are operating on autopilot, unconsciously applying outdated social maps that seem to regard humans as flat, hedonistic beings that must be cajoled and manipulated into buying things they don't really need. As the saying goes, "You'll know the tree by its fruit." If so, we might liken most of today's marketing to the fruit of a tree that has had raw chemicals dumped directly into its root system.

News Flash: media that derives from uninspiring intentions does not inspire people! Yes, such media may generate decent sales activity, especially among a mass of consumers who have slowly become habituated to our culture of myopia and shady ethics, but inspiration is not the only way to generate profits. Profits can also be generated through bank robberies and card tricks.

Three tastes that taste awful together

The flaws of our current mass-communication map can be broken down into three distinct mental fallacies. These fallacies represent areas of collective thinking where we, as communicators, habitually overlook or distort important information when making content and stylistic choices.

Communication Flaw #1:
The "Shallow Human" fallacy – We unconsciously adopt a view of the consumer as a physical body with a shallow, pleasure-seeking mind.

What about the soul or spirit? We rarely design media that respects our audience as a group of complex, multi-dimensional, spiritual beings with the same deep hopes, dreams, and problems as ourselves.

COMMUNICATION FLAW #2:

The "People-Are" fallacy – We unconsciously assume that our audience are composed of a homogenous group of people at roughly the same stage of mental development, with the same generic core values. As a result we fail to distinguish and respect very clear differences in values—and worldviews—that exist across audiences.

COMMUNICATION FLAW #3:

The "Scarcity" fallacy – We buy into the notion that there's not enough to go around. This places us in a state of perpetual insecurity and causes us to believe that we must manipulate others in order to survive. As a consequence, we learn to embrace all sorts of depressing communication tactics, including fear mongering, lying and poor listening.

Taken separately, each of these factors can poison our ability to inspire. Taken cumulatively, the impact is exponentially awful. Why? Because these three errors read as a sure-fire recipe for offending the very aspect of our audience that matters most: their *spirit.*

Inspiration in Action #1: The laugh behind the lie

Over the past decade, social satirists have come up with a clever new way of showing the absurdity of pop-media. By taking clips from a variety of thematically related news sources and splicing them together in quick rhythmic succession, they've learned to take spin out of context and show just how silly our national conversation can be. For a good example of this approach in action, watch virtually any episode of *The Daily Show* with Jon Stewart, or documentaries from activists Michael Moore and Robert Greenwald.

The gauntlet has been thrown

Our challenge as inspirational communicators and social leaders is to design communications that reach the human spirit. This means that we must speak to our audience with dignity and respect, giving them credit for being complex, multi-dimensional beings at a particular stage of development, living in a world with enough to go around for everyone. Not only must we integrate this understanding into every stage of the design process, but we must also authentically believe this to be true—we must have the strength of our convictions. If not, then this whole conversation becomes just another excuse to manipulate.

The great news is that when we do come from the correct mindset, our work is infinitely more powerful and the results we generate will seamlessly manifest on every level—material, mental and spiritual. The truth is powerful stuff. But, please don't shave your head and start singing "Kumbaya" just yet. We've got some serious work to do if we want to make these lofty ideas gain traction in the real world. Here are some major questions we must address:

- *If humans are "multi-dimensional," what are these dimensions and how do they interact to create the gestalt of human experience?*

- *How will dimensionality inform the way we design media and communications to ignite inspiration in our audiences?*

- *If people are psychologically progressing along specific developmental paths, what do these paths look like and why do they matter?*

We will soon review the Transformational Design® model, a groundbreaking design framework that explicitly addresses all of these questions and more. To frame the model with boring academic jargon, it is a phenomenological, existential, developmental model of human communication that can be applied to real-world communication challenges to create breakthrough results. Through this powerful new lens we will understand our audience more deeply and be able to strategically overcome any barriers they may have to allowing inspiration to naturally emerge.

Melting the iceberg of inspiration

To illustrate the relationship between Transformational Design® and traditional design, let's liken the realm of human inspiration to an iceberg (see Figure 1). As you can see, like any good iceberg, our "iceberg of inspiration" is composed almost entirely of ice that is hidden beneath the water's surface. We can't see it, but there it is—waiting to sink our ship.

Traditional communication design deals mostly with the tip of the iceberg—the sensory realm of words, visuals, symbols, logos, sounds, styles, textures, placement methods and strategies. By comparison, Transformational Design deals primarily with the hidden part, the part beneath the water. This is the realm of message *authenticity* and *personal relevance*. You can't directly see it or measure these attributes, but they are what give our messages absolutely any and all persuasive power.

When we combine traditional methods with the Transformational Design® methods, we will finally be firing on all cylinders—not just occasionally, but always. And the results we'll create will be uplifting to both our audience and our bottom line.

Two game-changing questions

Replacing old mental maps might sound like a lot of hard work, but it is actually just a matter of asking the right questions. In fact, there are only two fundamental questions that we must ask—and answer—before we can understand how to create messages that inspire all audiences. These questions represent two areas of fundamental insight into human nature that all great communicators intuitively possess.

    I. THE UNIVERSALS – *How are all people alike?*

        We must first understand the universal principles that tie all of us humans together, so that we can authentically engage the one source that unites us. Recognition of mankind's inherent unity is the experiential basis for inspiration.

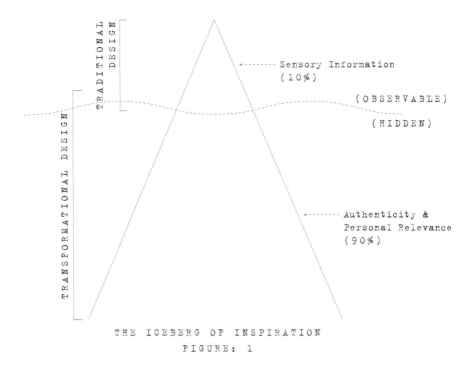

THE ICEBERG OF INSPIRATION
FIGURE: 1

2. THE DIFFERENCES – *How do people differ meaningfully?*
We must understand the core values of our audience so that we can frame messages in a way that resonates with their particular world-view. As we'll see, one's values evolve over time, forming a mental filter that largely determines whether or not our message is heard.

The content of this book has been strategically organized to thoroughly answer these two bold questions, and thus chart a more effective map for navigating the rocky shores of inspired communication. We'll use science, poetry, philosophy, spirituality, humor, and every other tool in the box to indelibly ingrain this new map into your brain. In Part I we'll need to do a little heavy lifting, but by the end of Part III you'll see that every single step was an important part of a highly practical journey into the uncharted recesses of our shared humanity, pregnant with the potential to completely transform the way we communicate in the service of our one shared life.

Part I.

THE UNIVERSALS: How are all people alike?

In Part I, we'll explore the anatomy of inspiration. To do this, we'll revisit some basic assumptions about what makes humans tick and redefine the experience of inspiration through a simple multi-dimensional lens. We'll get a feel for the barriers that habitually keep humans from feeling inspired and learn proven design strategies for overcoming these barriers.

← "WHY" IS HERE

CHAPTER 01

.....

THE ANATOMY OF INSPIRATION

.....

"Life happens when the tectonic power of your speech-less soul breaks through the dead habits of the mind."
- John Patrick Shanley

The first deadly mistake most communicators make is that they fail to appreciate the full depth and complexity of their target audience. This is bad news, indeed. Not only does it cause them to unwittingly offend those they seek to communicate with, but it also causes them, over time, to lose touch with the deeper, inspirational dimensions of their own being. It's a vicious, soul-killing cycle.

In this chapter we will revisit some of the fundamentals—the basic, intuitive, obvious stuff that most of us forgot once we got caught up in the rat race of fixed-rate mortgages and dental plans. It turns out that this basic stuff holds the hidden keys to unlocking untold powers of uplifting influence in all of us.

Three Dimensions of a Human Being

All humans simultaneously exist on three planes or dimensions: material, mental and spiritual. To understand how to create inspiration, we must understand the distinct qualities of each plane and grasp the complex dynamics through which they interact to produce human experience.

MATERIAL DIMENSION: Consists of the physical body and everything in the material universe. All material information is brought to the mind through the limited channel of the five senses. Material forms are characterized by constant change—growth, decay and renewal. This process can appear quite random and chaotic at times.

MENTAL DIMENSION: Consists of thoughts, feelings and ideas. These thoughts occur spontaneously and are usually referenced outward towards the material plane in an effort to control events and circumstances. Thought forms can change very quickly, but tend to have a recurring, patterned nature and a longer shelf-life than material forms. Thoughts are creative, and tend to occur within a specific (hidden) context based on certain (hidden) assumptions.

SPIRITUAL DIMENSION: Consists of pure potential. It is beyond time and space, therefore beyond change. It is the source of intelligence and life energy that underlies the mental and material realm, but cannot be directly perceived or measured. Because it is beyond time and space, the spiritual dimension is also non-dual—beyond all opposites. It cannot be understood with the mind, but it can be directly experienced by those willing to suspend thinking.

This three-dimensional view of human nature has shown up in religions, mythologies, and philosophies since nearly the beginning of recorded time, but rarely has it been strategically applied to solve practical communication challenges. Doing so gives us amazing insights.

Figure 2 on the opposite page has been created to visually represent this three dimensional structure of a human being. As you look it over, notice first that the three dimensions are represented by circles of ascending size, starting with the material dimension (body), moving through the transformational dimension (mind), and culminating with the causal dimension (spirit). According to common sense, this is the basic flow of human experience—sensory information transforms into thoughts which (sometimes) give way to spiritual experiences. However, the opposite flow is also conceivable; spiritual insights can cause changed mental attitudes that lead to tangible material outcomes. This model accounts for the possibility of both causal flows.

Also, please notice that the vertical axis on Figure 2 from body to spirit is represented by a decrease in temporality as we approach the causal

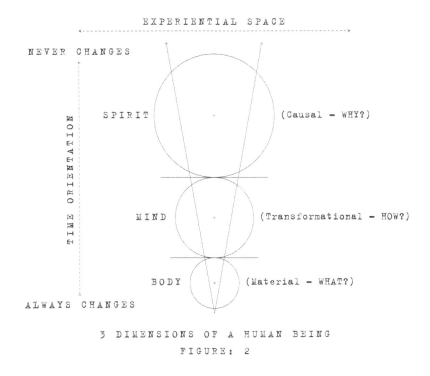

3 DIMENSIONS OF A HUMAN BEING
FIGURE: 2

plane. In other words, Einstein was right. Time *is* relative. On the material plane, time is vivid and urgent. On the causal (or spiritual) plane, time is totally non-existent. Between these two extremes, lies the fickle mind, for which time is either fast or slow depending on which dimension captures its immediate attention (material or spiritual).

Finally, please note that the horizontal axis represents experiential 'space.' The widening of circles as we ascend from the lowest physical plane (body) towards the highest causal plane (spirit) represents a dramatic increase in subjective experiential capacity. This means that a person experiences the least sense of subjective space when identifying with self as a physical body, and the most expanded sense when identifying with self as spirit. This choice is always made by the mind, which is itself located somewhere on the continuum between limitation and infinity.

So what's the point? The point is that humans are complex! We can be accurately described as multi-dimensional systems that span from constant change and renewal (cells of the body) to absolute stillness and peace (spirit). This might seem like an abstract, philosophical proposition right now, but you'll soon see that it has awesome implications for activating inspiration in the realm of ordinary everyday communication.

Humans are a matter of perspective

Based on this model, we humans can be observed from at least two fundamentally distinct perspectives. One perspective focuses on the observables: the physical body (with the unseen planes as secondary). An opposite vantage point views us as primarily spiritual beings (with material and mental planes as secondary). Depending on which perspective we choose, we will arrive at a fundamentally different conception of what the world is and what is the ultimate purpose of human existence. For fun, let's compare and contrast.

PERSPECTIVE #1: *Humans are material*

We are primarily physical beings struggling for survival with a limited time alive here on earth. The truth of life is danger, limitation and conflict. We have developed minds that give us the ability to think and reason. Our mind is our best asset for winning the endless battle against nature by overcoming the elements, attaining safety, and maximizing pleasure. There may or may not be some deeper 'spirit,' but this is

---

Inspiration in Action #2: Health is not a four letter word

Most medical doctors disregard things that cannot be measured (such as the mind and spirit). Unfortunately this lack of vision into hidden causal dimensions has left our medical establishment with woefully inadequate models for fostering sustainable health. But times are changing, thanks to an unprecedented health care crisis and many insightful doctors who have spoken out on the importance of taking a more holistic approach.

In his 1992 book *Ageless Body Timeless Mind*, Deepak Chopra did just this. By reinterpreting western medical data through a spiritual lens, Dr. Chopra helped to inspire a medical mind-body-spirit revolution that is unfolding still today.

basically irrelevant to survival issues at hand. Survival is the thing.

PERSPECTIVE #2: *Humans are spiritual*

We are primarily spiritual beings with an infinite and unchanging nature that is the one source of all life. Out of this one essential nature, we have created our physical bodies and the entire material universe. Our true hidden nature is unbounded unity. This truth is always available to everyone, but most people are so identified with the realm of thinking and doing that they've forgotten how to access it. By accessing it again we have the power to transform the material realm.

Pretty big difference, isn't it?

Believe it or not, I'm not here to prove that either point of view is correct. The fact is, all humans exist on all three planes and we ignore this truth at our own peril. We all must eat to keep our body alive, and we all must love to keep our spirit soaring. The purpose for bringing this grand distinction up is to start generating some deeper insight into the profound impact that our worldview may have on our ability to inspire others. Which perspective do you prefer? Even better, if you wanted to be the kind of person that could ignite the masses, which do you imagine would be most effective?

More implications of dimensionality

You'll find that once the dimensional model outlined in Figure 2 (page 15) sinks into your brain, it will become an indispensable part of the way your mind makes sense of the world. Like all good symbols, the reason it sticks in the head so well is that it's true. This simple symbol will provide powerful, resonant insights to help you relate to other humans in a way that pulls for a sense of commonality and unity.

Perhaps the most bizarre insight that this model reveals is that the mind is fundamentally a non-entity. With all of its thoughts and fears and hopes and wants, the mind is but a swirling transformational zone where material reality and spiritual reality meet. Does this concept seem a bit too lofty? Consider the following poem by William Blake:

```
We learn to believe a lie
When we see with and not through the eye
Which was born in a night
To perish in a night
When the soul slept in beams of light[1]
```

Now, please read this poem again, substituting the word "mind" for "eye." Go ahead...It works, doesn't it? If not artistically, certainly in theory. Can you imagine a mind without a body? What would you think about? Can you imagine a mind without a spirit? From where would you get insights and energy? The mind exists to transform spiritual reality into physical reality, and vice versa. Without either, it could not exist. If you are willing to seriously consider this, an amazing insight will soon follow: not only are you not your mind, but your mind has no power aside from that which you grant it. In fact, some invisible part of you is bigger than your mind and has been running the show since day one!

The unfortunate truth is that most of us are just as trapped in the reality of the mind as we are in the reality of the body. This has a lot of staggering implications. Not just for our ability to communicate with others, but for our ability to grasp the deeper meaning and purpose of life (to which the ability to communicate is highly related).

Any endeavor that seeks to understand human persuasion and inspiration without looking beyond the mind is missing the boat. It is for this reason that thousands of hard-working, intelligent students graduate from advanced Ph.D. psychology programs every year with little or no genuine wisdom or insight into other humans. They're looking in the wrong place. Wisdom and insight *enter* minds, but they do not *come from* minds. The mind is just a bridge, a vaporous entity.

We're also looking in the wrong place when we search for the meaning of human life and inspiration in the body (our own or someone else's). The body is just a temporary tool of the universal, or spiritual realm. Your family doctor may balk at this suggestion, and for good reason: he or she probably spent a lot of time in school learning that the body is the be-all and end-all of human existence.

"Are you telling me that my doctor is naive?! Are you saying that my psychologist is ignorant?!" No, not necessarily. I'm speaking in generalities and I'm making a general point with huge implications for a person's ability to understand their self and relate to others. It isn't new—it's a point that nearly every great poet, mystic, musician, and artistic visionary has made since culture began. Here it is, yet again: the essence of who we are cannot be localized in either our bodies or in our minds. The essence of who we are is beyond knowing. And it is this "beyond knowing" part that holds the key to unlocking our power to generate inspiration on a massive scale and to solve every problem of human existence.

Who do you think you are?

Once we choose to seriously consider that man is a primarily spiritual being pretending to be physical, everything starts to make sense. *Why do people still buy those obnoxious Hummer SUV's? How could anyone have voted for George W. Bush? Why can't I stop eating these friggin' Twinkies?* Questions that once seemed baffling become crystal clear. As individuals and as a species, we are in the grips of a fabulous identity crisis. Having bought into the notion that we are primarily physical beings, we feel powerless and terrified. Without a firm existential footing, we invent bizarre beliefs in which to hide. From these "safe" mental havens, we band together for a while to project our fears outward and attain, hopefully, a fleeting sense of security and peace. But all beliefs are ultimately smokescreens masking a deeper anxiety, and all anxiety must eventually surface.

A great communicator is someone who liberates people from these rigid mental havens and helps the smoke clear. A great communicator understands that all mental forms are spiritual prisons and gently invites us to unlock the doors and step outside to a world where infinity is a fact, and scarcity an illusion. Inspiration is the feeling of freedom and joy that arises from the realization that who we really are is beyond all limiting beliefs.

Inspiration in Action #3: Oprah's pop-spirituality empire

Oprah is one of our country's most successful people and a source of inspiration to millions. Why has her success been so immense and enduring? Some people believe it has to do with her triumphant life story...but they've got it exactly backwards. Her triumphant life story is a result, not a cause. The real reason for Oprah's success relates to her personal insight into the spiritual dimension and her willingness to visibly champion it. Watch any show, or simply visit her web site (www.oprah.com), and you'll notice that almost every piece of media she sponsors eloquently argues for the spiritual basis of human being, and does so in a way that isn't offensive. The moral of the story? A guilt-free argument for spirituality can really make you popular! How do you like me so far?

Inspired communication = accessing essence

If mankind's true essence is spiritual, then mankind's essential state is inspiration. If we want to inspire people, we must set ourselves to the task of helping people access this deeper layer of self. This is the secret of all great communicators. We don't need to argue with other's minds, we don't need to cajole or persuade them. No. What we must do is tactfully invite others to experience this one truth behind all mental forms.

They say the truth will set you free—and they're right. But the tricky thing to understand here is that the truth we're talking about is not factual truth, it's spiritual truth. Such truth cannot be forced down someone's throat the way we force our kids to eat soggy broccoli. It must be earned through the twin powers of authenticity and empathy. The reason that these traits are so powerful is that they gently direct the attention upwards towards the spiritual realm. This is a delicate procedure that cannot be easily accomplished by someone who is operating from a hard-core mistrust of all things metaphysical.

Along with "love," "integrity" is probably the most widely misunderstood word in the English language. Most people view integrity as congruence between what a person says and what a person does. True integrity goes much deeper. True integrity is congruence between what a person is (spirit), what a person thinks (mind) and what they do (body). When a person is integrated like this on every plane, we call this structural integrity. It's a powerful state indeed. In practice, no one can maintain this sort of integrity all the time, but the humility and discipline to persistently seek it is itself enough—over time—to lift one from the realm of survival and give them power to transform life in the material world.

A love note for the skeptics

As I cover this metaphysically oriented material, I suspect that a certain number of tough-minded readers may be turned off by spiritual terminology. That's fine. Like wine, a little skepticism can be healthy, but too much can make you dense. I've found that trying to open the mind of a hard-boiled skeptic is like trying to teach a pig to sing—you just end up frustrating both yourself and the pig.

For those of you on the fence, please know that the assumption of man's spiritual nature has nothing necessarily to do with any organized religion or Kool-Aid-drinking cult. It can be viewed as primarily a pragmatic assumption that affords us unparalleled access to energies that we can use to leverage results on the mental and material planes. If this explanation still doesn't float your boat, I've put together a table below. It contains a list of non-creepy synonyms for the word "spirit." Feel free to pick and choose, substituting the word that you find least offensive for the remainder of our time together.

Non-creepy synonyms for 'spirit'
mojo, essence, universal goo, self, ghost in the machine, acausal connecting principle, quantum field, higher self, life force, new age pap, breath, vital force, inner pinball wizard, energy, intelligence, tao, chi, being, nothingness, the great void, eternal self, non-local field, energy, higher consciousness, ontological ground, that thing, my happy place, juju, animating force, generative social field, renewable inner energy source, love

CHAPTER 02

·····

EXISTENTIAL LEVERAGING 101

·····

"Problems cannot be solved from the same level of consciousness that created them." - Albert Einstein

If we define inspiration as what happens when a person's attention identifies with the spiritual dimension, then our goal as an inspirational communicator becomes clear: we must craft communications that compel our
audiences to release the barriers that keep their own spiritual nature from
present-moment awareness. Inspiration is the most natural process in the
world, but it can't be forced. Trying to force inspiration is like trying to
force someone to love you—it's futile and more than a trifle depressing.

What does this mean for us as communicators? It means that we can
only inspire someone who is willing to be inspired. It also means that our
main task is to design communications in a way that strategically develops
a sense of *willingness* for inspiration in our audiences. If we can do this, we
will have created a powerful context in which inspiration will effortlessly
emerge, and we will have also made a lot of new friends.

The power of inspiration to move people into sustained action derives
from a principle called "existential leveraging" (see Figure 3 on page 24).
This principle proposes that there is a hierarchical relationship among
levels within the human being, with the spiritual dimension holding the
highest degree of power or leverage over the total bio-psycho-spiritual
system. According to this principle, one can only effect change at a given
level by accessing energies from the next highest level. Failure to understand this principle is at the heart of almost every failed initiative (public
and private) in the history of mankind.

Billions of dollars and man-hours are wasted every year by organizations with talented employees and good intentions. Movie moguls pro-
mote movies that no one likes, ad execs create campaigns that fall flat,

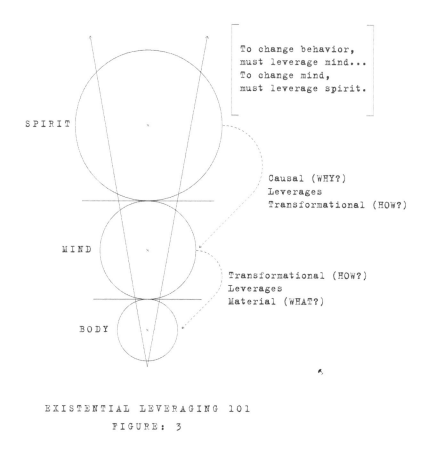

To change behavior,
must leverage mind...
To change mind,
must leverage spirit.

SPIRIT

Causal (WHY?)
Leverages
Transformational (HOW?)

MIND

Transformational (HOW?)
Leverages
Material (WHAT?)

BODY

EXISTENTIAL LEVERAGING 101
FIGURE: 3

politicians evangelize promises that no one believes. So much of this waste could be avoided if leaders were just a little more savvy about the law of leveraging and the hidden dynamics of inspiration.

The perils of poor leveraging

To illustrate poor leveraging in a relatable way, let's look at a topic close to almost every American heart: obesity.

Imagine that you are one hundred pounds overweight. Your doctor commands you to lose the flab. Well, dangerous and temporary "miracle" surgeries aside, that's going to be impossible to achieve without first changing your mindset. To transform the physical dimension we must go up one level to the mind, right?

Great, so how do we change the mind? Perhaps we buy a good diet book, hire a personal trainer, purchase a treadmill, and buy some new sweatpants and a fuzzy purple headband. We're ready—we're really going to do it this time! And we do well, for a little while...and then what?

The inspiration dries up. French fries and chocolate muffins start looking heavenly. The personal trainer annoys us. Our mind veers back into dead-end thinking. *What's the point? Who am I kidding? Diets don't work. Maybe I've got a problem with my glands...*

Soon we're sitting on the couch again, eating chips, eyeing that new "Hollywood Miracle Diet" infomercial with a soul-suffocating mixture of hopefulness and disdain.

Lather, rinse, repeat.

What's the problem here?

The problem is that we tried to leverage the body with the mind, but we were unable to get leverage over the mind itself. Why? Because the mind, like the body, gets its orders from a higher source: the spirit. It's not enough to work on just the mind. We must go deeper. We must somehow overcome the hidden barrier that keeps us trapped into mental identification.

In fact, if we look more closely at what happened, we'll see that whatever genuine energy and inspiration we had actually came from beyond the mind. For a brief moment at least, the urgency of the situation and the yearning for health pushed us to disengage from habitual thinking. We became charged with inspiration and ready to go, but we couldn't keep our footing and, eventually, we fell back down into the world of bodies and impulsive thoughts of fast food and ice cream.

I've yet to meet one person who hasn't fallen prey to this dynamic in one form or another—with food, sex, cigarettes, money, work, or some other fixation. The take home point is this: slavish life habits, no matter how brutish and compelling, can only be maintained through a lack of insight into the spiritual dimension that lies behind the mind, and a lack of willingness to fully experience this dimension.

Taking it up a notch

Now, let's make things even more global and dire. Let's say you live on a planet where the ice caps are melting and the food supply is getting poisoned due to the poor living habits of the dominant species. Your problem is fundamentally a material one, right? You need to get that species to stop dumping toxins into the ground and air. So you pass a bunch of new laws designed to fix the problem and you create highly visible new campaigns designed to persuade the beings on this planet to behave differently.

And a lot of life forms on this planet get excited for awhile—but nothing changes.

So, what's the problem?

The problem in this situation is ultimately the same as for the overweight person above, but on a larger scale: the species on this (hypothetical) planet has lost its ability to identify with the causal realm and cannot overcome its inertia. As long as this species stays focused on solutions that rely on changing laws and behaviors (material dimension) and trying to cajole or persuade others (mental dimension), it will lack energetic leverage to create a genuine sustainable transformation.

Inspiration in Action #4: A painfully inspiring truth

In his Oscar-winning film "An Inconvenient Truth" Al Gore did a wonderful job of demonstrating the horrible hell that humans will create if we don't dramatically limit our global carbon emissions. Unfortunately he spent far less time creating an inspired, credible vision for our collective future. The result? His message reached only those uncommonly brave souls who were willing to stare despair in the eyes without blinking. To ignite massive, transformational environmental inspiration we need to focus less on problems and more on compelling visions for the future. We must start designing media and messaging campaigns that cause the American people to start viewing the sustainability movement as the unprecedented personal and collective opportunity that it truly is.

The hidden physics of transformation

Please understand that we're not talking wacky stuff here. We're talking mechanics. We're talking physics. If you throw a ball, it will eventually fall. If you heat water, it will eventually boil. If you inspire humans, they will eventually transform—and not a minute sooner.

When Einstein said, "A problem cannot be solved from the same level of consciousness that created it," he was saying essentially the same thing. It's a simple truth and it's plain to see for anyone brave enough to consider that there's more to life than meets the eye. This is wonderful news, because this insight gives us the kind of access to inspire on a massive scale that has never existed in the history of our species.

It turns out that all these glittery toys we've created for the mass creation and distribution of information (internet, television, movies, video games, etc.) will come in quite handy once we start using them for authentic purposes. Placed in a larger context, Transformational Design is really just a way to design media and communications so that they can finally start serving the source of life, or (if you prefer) 'spirit.'

Three ways to move a rock

Given the concept of existential leveraging, we will now redefine communication in accordance with our 3-dimensional model. It turns out that there are just three basic types of communication. Reviewing Figure 4 on page 29, you'll notice that we've taken two-dimensional models of a human being and juxtaposed them. In this scenario, we see that Person A wishes to get Person B to move rock C. Easy enough.

Looking closer, you'll also notice lines connecting Persons A and B on three distinct levels: Body-to-Body, Mind-to-Mind, and Spirit-to-Spirit. These lines represent three different paths by which Person A can attempt to engage Person B in order to get the rock moved.

COMMUNICATION PATH #1:

(Body-to-Body) is called FORCE. Under this approach, Person A uses his body and/or threats of bodily harm to force Person B's body to move the rock. This type of communication is the dominant mode used by dictators, terrorists, militants, and other unpleasant people.

COMMUNICATION PATH #2:

(Mind-to-Mind) is called PERSUASION. Under this approach, Person A uses his mind (by reasoning and cajoling) to persuade Person B's mind to make Person B's body move the rock. This is the dominant form of communication in our culture today, and it can be seen most visibly in the communication patterns of marketing executives, salesmen, lawyers, politicians, and other clever people.

COMMUNICATION PATH #3:

(Spirit-to-Spirit) is called INSPIRATION. Under this approach, Person A uses his spirit to move Person B's spirit to inspire Person B's mind to motivate Person B's body to move the rock. This is the predominant method of communication used by revolutionaries, speakers, artists, and visionaries throughout human history, such as Martin Luther King Jr., John F. Kennedy, Buddha, and Gandhi.

All three communication paths will accomplish the same stated material task—moving the rock. But, due to the law of leveraging, each approach will have a different long-term impact upon person A and person B, and create vastly different results on unseen dimensions. Let's briefly look at these and compare.

Forcing the rock

The easiest thing about forcing is that, at first, it requires very little mental effort for the forcer (Person A). Unfortunately, this ease comes at a great long-term cost. Because the forced individual (Person B) is being engaged only on the physical level, his or her unacknowledged mental and spiritual dimensions tend to retract, generating resistance. This resistance grows

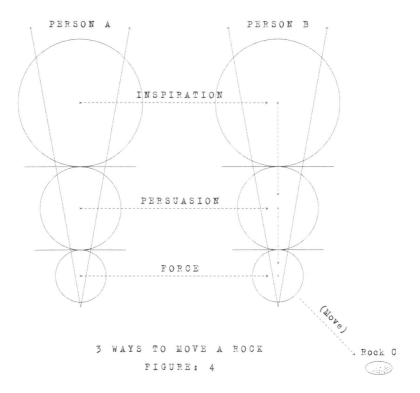

PERSON A   PERSON B

INSPIRATION

PERSUASION

FORCE

(Move)

3 WAYS TO MOVE A ROCK   Rock C

FIGURE: 4

over time, necessitating the need for greater and greater force by Person A.

Can you remember being forced to do something? Can you remember forcing *yourself* to do something? Was it fun? Most people remember much of their schooling with a special horror and revile the idea of being put into a classroom again. Why? Because militant teachers forced the joy of learning right out of them. The most vivid stories come from those infamous tales of parochial school halls where authoritarian figures were purported to use wooden rulers as instruments of divine instruction. People educated in this sort of environment seldom enjoy school (or religion) once they grow up and enter the secular world.

In the end, we find that forcing is the most inefficient form of communication possible because it denies the deepest aspects of the human being and leads to permanent negative long-term consequences such as bitterness, negativity, and the calcification of cynicism in all involved.

Persuading the rock

Persuasion affords the communicator much better leverage to accomplish desired tasks than forcing, without the disastrous side effects. Because persuaders access the target individual on the level of mind, the actions that result usually generate much less resistance and have a longer shelf-life. From the communicator's point of view, persuasion is infinitely more efficient than forcing, because the time spent persuading can motivate behaviors that may continue indefinitely.

Persuasion is particularly popular in the United States because it resonates with the basic cultural and economic tenets of free-market capitalism, and also because most of us have simply grown accustomed to it. If you want to learn about persuading, just walk the aisle of the sales and marketing section of any bookstore. Better yet, take a gander at the ever-popular self-help aisle—you'll find self-persuasion techniques for every occasion. The persuasion business has infiltrated every corner of our society, and business is always booming.

Despite its advantages, persuasion has some insidious limitations. These limitation are often hidden to the naked eye, but always manifest in one form or another. Because it originates from the mind, persuasion implies that either: 1) there is no spiritual component to either party, or 2) there is a spiritual component, but it's not important. Remember our definition of inspiration? Inspiration is what happens when a person identifies with the spiritual dimension of their own being. This isn't advanced calculus, here. Whenever we implicitly or explicitly deny the spiritual component of ourselves and others, we will not be inspired, nor will they. Denial of the spiritual dimension leads not only to a lack of inspiration, but to poor leveraging and a whole host of fear-based communication tactics, such as dishonesty, fear mongering and manipulation. By using persuasive tactics, we can often get people excited about our offering. If we're good, we might even get filthy rich. But at what cost?

Inspiration in Action #5: Transparent seduction for skeptics

As most single women will tell you, all men have an ulterior motive. In fact, this tendency among men has made many otherwise available women jaded to the point that they won't trust anyone, no matter how authentic. In my days as a roving single, one terrific strategy that I found for overcoming this trust barrier with skeptical women was to sometimes humorously disclose my motive right off the bat: "I must confess, your lack of trust is making it hard for me to secretly manipulate you." Most would find this sort of paradoxical directness funny and refreshing. I use this tactic still today when writing copy for media that caters to particularly guarded audiences. Try it. It works.

Inspiring the rock

As you've probably guessed, inspiration offers the best leverage and generates the most sustainable results from the least effort. With inspiration, we access our own spiritual dimension to activate the corresponding dimension within our 'target.' This energy mobilizes the other person's mind to generate curiosity and enthusiasm for our offering, which can then be channeled into the desired physical actions. Because the entire three-dimensional human body-mind-spirit system has been incorporated, the experience is intrinsically fun and energizing. Also, because action ultimately originates from the unchanging 'causal' dimension, the shelf-life of influence can be infinite.

So what's the rub? Why doesn't everyone just engage in inspiration all the time then?

Two words: cynicism and resignation.

The battle to inspire and be inspired is really the battle to trust again, to release our cynicism so that a deeper truth can shine through. This battle cannot be won overnight, but neither can it be lost—not if we're earnestly willing to fight it. Remember: the mind has no power except that which we give it. All we really must do is stand tall and remind our drama-loving cortex who's really running the show.

Remembering inspiration

Have you ever fallen madly in love? Have you ever had an amazing conversation that kept you up for hours without the need for food or sleep? Has a brilliant piece of music ever moved you to tears? Have you ever felt transported by the eloquence of a gifted orator? Have you felt ineffably connected to a stranger in a moment of crisis? Have you ever been entranced by the timeless charms of a chubby baby?

These are just a few faces of inspiration. It's infinite—in fact, it's the literal experience of infinity, of that unbounded experiential dimension that each of us carries innate. Socially, it is the recognition that we share this infinite something with each other. Is it hard to imagine that you could incorporate this kind of experience into your everyday life as a duty-bound adult? Yes, perhaps—but that doesn't mean it's impossible. Not only is it possible, but it's necessary and it's inevitable.

We live in a mind-blowing time where a critical mass of people are becoming disenchanted with the old ways and are actively seeking new ways, or contexts, for living. We seem to be collectively unwilling to continue pretending as though there is nothing more to us than just a temporary body and a pleasure-seeking mind. We seem to be craving something deeper and more sustainable, not just in terms of our outer environment, but also our inner environments. We seem to be ready to reclaim our birthright—the natural state of inspiration that all those years of forcing and persuading bred right out of us.

As we move forward, we'll learn that our biggest barrier to reclaiming this higher ground and seizing this opportunity rests not in the world outside us, but in our inner willingness to let go of the cynicism that we've accrued to protect ourselves from an apparently dangerous, threatening world. Martin Luther King's "fierce urgency of now" is but the recognition that we are bigger than our piddling fears, and are finally willing to yield to a deeper voice that knows the way. This voice is inspiration, and whenever we meet we either share it or lose it together.

Step to, soldier!

In the next chapter we'll bring this lofty conversation back down to earth by exploring the practical implications that this model has for anyone tasked with creating inspirational campaigns. We'll find that in order to design breakthrough media and messaging, we must pay special attention to overcoming the perceptual and mental barriers of our target audience. What's more, we'll learn that one of the most vital tools for accomplishing this rests in an often overlooked place—our own intentions.

CHAPTER 03

. . . . .

DESIGNING INSPIRATION

. . . . .

"Any sufficiently developed technology is indistinguishable from magic." — G.K. Chesterton

Ask any cognitive psychologist: perception happens fast! When we open our eyes each morning, we encounter a world populated by people, places and things that seem to occur independent of us, but it's just an illusion. The truth is that by the time our brain begins to make the slightest order of the energies that bombard our senses at any given moment, we've already made many subjective interpretive choices at a deeper level.

Put more bluntly, we are constantly making the world up. The world we experience as we take in the landscape is a product of our imagination— simple sensory data stitched together by our mind into a tapestry of meaning built upon past learning. Now, with this thought in mind, let's revisit the dimensional model. As you'll see, this simple graphic is actually an elegant strategic tool that we can use to help us conceptually slow down time and get a structural view of the multidimensional dynamics of human experience, real-time, as they occur.

Please see Figure 5 on the top of page 36. You'll notice that we've placed the dimensional model on its side so that it reads from left to right, starting with the body and ending with the spirit. The area on the left side of the diagram is the external world of forms and objects. In order for this external stimulus to inspire, it must pass (from left to right) through each successive layer, or dimension, and access the hidden source of inspiration itself. At each leg of the journey the inspirational stimulus must pass through certain key thresholds in order to reach the experiential promised land of inspiration.

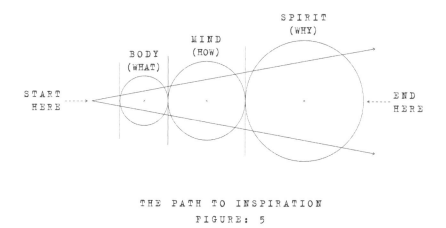

THE PATH TO INSPIRATION
FIGURE: 5

Introducing the concept of filters

It is useful to think of the transitional space between each dimension as a filter. Each filter has unique characteristics and responds to different types of information. The *sensory filter* refers to the transitional zone between the external world and one's immediate perception; this filter responds mostly to captivating sensory data. The *mental filter* refers to the transitional zone between immediate perception and deeper cognition; this filter responds mostly to data related to the perceived personal relevance of the message or stimulus. Finally, the *spiritual filter* refers to the mysterious experiential zone where a thought becomes a reflection of something beyond the mind, or an experience of the transcendent; this filter responds strongly to data related to message authenticity.

Although we're portraying this as a linear time sequence of action, starting with the body and leading towards the spirit, it's worth pointing out that this is actually a vast oversimplification. It seems that what's really happening when a stimulus makes its way through these barriers has everything to do with which particular dimension the observer chooses to place his/her attention on: physical, mental, or spiritual. All stimuli can be said to exist on all three dimensions, but most people usually only allow themselves to observe the spiritual dimension for certain safe predetermined stimuli, such as specific religious symbols, loved ones, and works of art.

A great communicator can use this understanding of the dynamics of perception to strategically direct their audience's awareness to the less traveled, spiritual recesses of mind. This is the sort of communication mastery that legendary orators consistently demonstrate. For a modern illustration, look no further than President Barack Obama. Did you happen to see his career-launching speech at the Democratic National Convention in 2004? If not, please go on-line and watch it (www.youtube.com). You'll witness an inspirational master engaging and overcoming the mental and spiritual filters of his audience with otherworldly skill and grace. This grace has little to do with political affiliation, and everything to do with authenticity and insight into the transformational dynamics of language, context, and communication.

A love story for the ages

At first, the 'filter' concept might seem overly abstract, but don't be fooled. Overcoming filters is the most natural, relatable process in the world. Let's take one universally cherished example—falling in love. The generic Hollywood romantic myth goes something like this:

Girl sees boy. Girl speaks to boy, finds him charming. Girl and boy start dating and get to know one another. Things really heat up, until girl finds out about boy's wayward past. Doubts and fears surface. Will the boy hurt her? Boy grovels and serenades girl, tries to win her trust. In a fit of passion, girl finally decides to trust boy and take a chance. She lets go, falls madly. They kiss, embrace and live happily ever after. Fade out. The End.

A touching story isn't it? After you wipe the tears of joy away, let's take the fun out of it, and look it at it through our new lens:

Girl's sees appealing boy stimulus. Sensory filter opens. This captivating stimulus motivates girl to slightly open mental filter. Girl engages boy on a mental level and discovers deep congruence of values and resonance with personal goals. Mental resonance activates buried pain from girl's past. Should she release cynicism and open her spiritual filter to him? Girl decides that boy stimulus is authentic and allows spiritual filter to open fully, flooding her mind/body system with inspiration. Fade out. The End.

Not as romantic, perhaps, but equally true. The bottom line is that any inspiration is a result of openness to spiritual energies, and we can foster this type of openness only when we follow the rules of engagement. The rules of engagement are as follows: senses give way to thoughts, which give way to inspiration.

A roadmap to inspiration

How can we apply this model to solve real world communication challenges? Broadly speaking, we can use the dimensional model as a schematic representation of the path our communications must take in order to access the inner reaches of our audiences. We can then set strategic design goals and checklists based upon this dimensional structure. This is the core essence of the Transformational Design™ process.

Figure 6 (on page 39) is literally a roadmap for accessing inspiration. It clearly spells out each step our message must take in order to reach the spiritual promised land. The trick to creating inspirational media is grasping how to strategically design communications that can access deeper dimensions of our audience's perception by effortlessly calling upon them to open each successive filter in response to our message.

The truly revolutionary idea here is that when we take the time to break it down, the creative process of designing inspiration into our communications can now be scientific and systematic. However, in the interests of full disclosure, I must confess that a full scientific research agenda for this model has yet to be developed and tested. But never you worry! A deep grasp of cognitive psychology, existential philosophy and systems theory, coupled with years of practice as a writer and speaker have offered me many penetrating, practical insights into the basic principles that guide the operation of each filter. You will know that these principles are correct when you witness how well they work in your own life.

Design hurdle #1: overcoming the sensory filter

The design goal at the initial stage of the inspiration process is simply to capture someone's senses. Our senses are drawn to the most

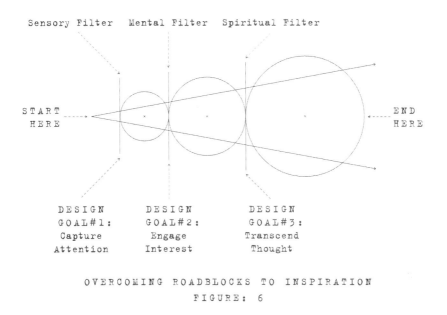

Sensory Filter   Mental Filter   Spiritual Filter

START
HERE

END
HERE

DESIGN
GOAL#1:
Capture
Attention

DESIGN
GOAL#2:
Engage
Interest

DESIGN
GOAL#3:
Transcend
Thought

OVERCOMING ROADBLOCKS TO INSPIRATION
FIGURE: 6

pleasing, threatening, or surprising stimuli from our immediate environment: cute things, cuddly things, colorful things, loud things, shiny things, pretty things, etc. This proclivity has been hard-wired into our physical makeup through eons of evolution.

Successful sense capturing requires an instinctive understanding of the laws of aesthetics and the vital role that balance, rhythm and texture play in creating the gestalt of perception. Ideally, a well-constructed campaign will seamlessly meld media type, design and placement in a way that effortlessly captures the attention of a specifically targeted audience.

Creating captivating design aesthetics is a fascinating topic that has been well covered in a multitude of prior sources, so I won't try to rehash all of them here.[2] Instead, I will offer up one unique bit of advice for visual designers that I've yet to hear properly referenced in popular design literature: always strive to know the core values of your target audience. Why? Because by knowing the core values of your audience, you will be able to intuitively predict their aesthetic preferences with remarkable clarity. (In Part II, we'll discuss this topic in intimate detail, spelling out specific stages of value development that exist across potential target audiences.)

Design hurdle #2:overcoming the mental filter

Our design goal at this stage of the process is to stoke our audience's curiosity and get them thinking. The pathway to mental engagement leads through the portal of *personal relevance*. The mind is a scanning device that is constantly assessing environmental cues to determine their relevance to pre-existing goals. If we can frame our message in a way that seems highly relevant to our target audience's personal hopes and goals, they will invariably open their mental filter and give our message strong consideration.

How do we strategically design a sense of personal relevance? This is where empathy and perspective-taking abilities reign supreme. We must seek to understand the world through our audience's eyes and cater our message directly to what they value most. To this end, expert communicators are usually skilled in the art of scientifically applying some or all of the following powerful rhetorical tools and tactics: *situational framing, value framing, problem-creating, personal recognition, questioning, resonant metaphors* and *storytelling*. (*Quick note:* The following lists are meant to give you just a brief, general overview of each filter-opening tactic. We will revisit each of them in a more applied, strategic fashion in Part II of this book.)

SITUATIONAL FRAMING: Once you've captured their senses, the most immediate way to get someone's mind working is to draw their attention to the specific environment (time and place) in which the communication is happening. "Do you come here often?" is a clichéd pick-up line from the era of hairy chests and polyester slacks, but it demonstrates a principle that still rings true: to establish mental rapport, we must first make certain that our audience is mentally present. Skillful questions that direct attention to the present situation are a great way to accomplish this.

Situational framing can occur through any medium—print, television, the internet, etc. The trick is to imagine the situation in which your target audience will encounter your message and decipher their purpose for being in that particular situation. With this knowledge we can craft our message so that it speaks to these specific situational factors. If it is a television commercial, what station and show will it be airing on? What can we infer about people who are watching that particular show? Are these people watching in order to attain investment advice? Good, we can use that. Are these people watching to escape the tedium of unemployment? Good, we can use that too. Do we expect that these people are sick and tired of loud commercials? Good, that might work just fine...

The possibilities are endless. The point is that we want to get our listeners to see that we understand, in a very intimate way, where they are coming from. Situational framing provides a fabulous launching point for engaging deeper mental access.

VALUE FRAMING: To create a very deep sense of personal relevance, we should seek to frame our message so that it speaks to our audience's core values. People's values create a powerful but hidden framework that determines whether or not something is important to them. Effective value framing causes value resonance—a sense of deep harmony between audience and message that dramatically raises mental energies.

The first key to effective value framing is (drum roll, please) to know your audience's values. Sound obvious? The fact is, most communicators have little or no insight into their audience's values. Even worse, they falsely believe that they do! Lacking a specific understanding of how others view the world, most of us unconsciously project our own values onto others. This is a sure-fire way to bore people and keep their mental filters slammed shut!

The second key to effective framing is to apply value frames *artfully*. As with actual painting frames, value frames should never call attention to themselves. Subtlety is the key. For example, let's assume your audience values financial prosperity above almost everything else. It's probably not a good idea to say flat out, "Don't you think money is the most important thing in life?" You might get a good laugh and bonus point for honesty, but you won't be taken seriously. A more effective approach might be to ask "Aren't you tired of people trying to take your hard-earned money? Don't you want to avoid the guilt of do-gooders and increase your net worth?" In this instance you've implied the importance of money, without making it so obvious. This person will be much more likely to feel like you understand them and will want to hear more. Subtlety is vital.

PROBLEM-CREATING: People love to pretend that they hate their problems. But without problems we would all be jobless and bored. Our minds are problem-solving machines. Expert communicators recognize this mental principle and strategically create problems for their audience to consider. But be forewarned: to successfully engage the mental filter, these problems must be framed in a way that represents a true and imminent threat to something that the audience holds dear. The listener's perceived self interest is paramount. Also, be sure to only raise problems for which you will eventually offer a genuine, concrete solution. Raising unsolvable problems simply makes people feel bad, and will not win you any new friends.

PERSONAL RECOGNITION: People just love to see and hear their own names, and will never tire of receiving personal acknowledgement. Strictly speaking, personal recognition is a form of situational framing in which the situation is customized to include a specific individual. This is a big challenge when our message is broadcast for a large, unspecified audience. In 'generic' mass campaigns, the trick is to find a sincere way to recognize and acknowledge the particular kind of person that constitutes your target audience. This requires a knowledge of specific audience types, a topic we'll later expand upon later.

QUESTIONING: From Socrates to Freud, questions have long been the secret favorite tool of all advanced persuasive communicators. The right question will stop a person's mind dead in its tracks and

---

Inspiration in Action #6: What's the matter with California?

Most progressives look with dismay at the dominance of the right-wing cable stronghold FOX news. But here's the deal: FOX news has been successful for a good reason—they know their audience and they are brilliant at framing news stories in a way that resonates with their audience's core values. The result? FOX has consistently high ratings and appears trustworthy to millions of well-meaning, but relatively unreflective Americans. Here's the good news: there's no reason that a similar value-framing strategy couldn't be designed into the mainstream media to inspire audiences to develop more life-serving frames of reference. Those of you who may object to such 'manipulative' tactics, please remember that all concepts are value-laden, even the notion of 'objectivity'. Authenticity requires the humility to admit that true objectivity is objectively impossible.

---

redirect it towards a realm of new possibilities. Remember: our superordinate goal is to develop a *willingness* for inspiration in our audiences. Used in conjunction with the other tools (value framing, problem creating, etc.) questions are the quickest way to do so.

One advanced tactic is to strategically ask questions that direct the listener's awareness to present life problems. The questioner can then use follow-up questions to systematically uncover hidden implications of these problems until the listener recognizes an urgent need for a new solution that they don't currently possess.[3] The process of developing *problems* into *urgent needs* deeply engages the mind, and directs the audience's attention towards the realm of unseen possibilities. From this state of openness, inspiration is a proverbial stone's throw away.

RESONANT METAPHORS: A secret, highly creative shortcut for mentally engaging others is to frame or embed your message with metaphors that resonate with their current world view. Does your audience view life as a winner-take-all *game*? A *battle* to the finish? A *test* of one's worth? Exploring and engaging your audience's preferred metaphors can lead to profoundly creative and insightful visual, auditory and verbal design possibilities.

But how can we possibly know our audience's favorite metaphors? We must first understand their core values. Research has shown that people's values correlate with certain key global metaphors. For example, people who value rugged individualism and strategy are very likely to view the world as a game. On the other hand, people who value piety, and sacrifice are more likely to view the world as a test.

STORYTELLING: A good story, well told, has a hypnotic effect that absorbs audiences to an unparalleled level of mental engagement. Just the words, "Once upon a time..." can act as a trigger provoking a dream-like trance across large masses. Why? Because, as humans, it's in our mental DNA. Stories form the mental threads that we use to weave the very tapestry of time and space that we call 'reality.'

A great storyteller gently grabs these threads, weaving them into new mind-bending patterns that leave listeners entranced. A great storyteller can also artfully embed all of the rhetorical elements outlined above (value-framing, questions, etc.) into their narrative without eliciting defensiveness or skepticism in their audience. As we'll discuss in the next section, the storytelling captivates the mind, but its the story theme or "payoff" that delivers the inspiration.

Design hurdle #3: overcoming the spiritual filter

Once we've gotten attention and engaged the mind, our design goal is to inspire our audience to experience or identify with their own spiritual essence. This requires that we invite them to experience our message differently. Our design challenge is to cultivate a moment in which the audience keeps their attention on the stimulus (media, speech, etc.) while releasing their need to judge or analyze. In other words, they must willingly suspend their critical faculties, without tuning us out or going unconscious. This is a deep shift in mental processing that can be tricky to elicit.

The vast majority of messages in our world never even come close to accomplishing this goal. People and campaigns that succeed become legendary. In fact, genuine inspiration is such a priceless commodity that hucksters quite often wear a mask of authenticity to attain social leverage, and uncritical audiences often pretend to be inspired by their masks. As a result of such mischief, many practical 'worldly' types have become so jaded that they've chosen to regard inspiration itself as a grand hoax.

When the smoke clears, we see that inspiration is real and that it can be accessed according to some basic spiritual filter laws. There are two fundamental principles that we must grasp (and apply) if we wish to design messages that consistently overcome the spiritual filter in our audiences: 1) the principle of authenticity, and 2) the principle of context. The first relates to our intentions for communicating, and the second relates to our tactics for doing so.

1) The Principle of Authenticity

Trust is the fuel for inspiration. People will never open their spiritual filter (read: release mental resistance) if they do not trust you. Why not? Because they don't want to get hurt! Existentially speaking, the mind is a tool that we have developed in order to avoid feeling pain. People who manipulate by persuading and forcing others for their own ends cause a lot of pain in this world. Only genuine trust can create a strong enough energetic context from which our audiences will be able to let go of this painful past and open up again.

Question: What's the best way to gain our audience's trust?
Answer: Deserve it by being authentic.

Simple, right? Not always. Being authentic is easier said than done. It requires seamless integration of awareness upon all three dimensions at once (aka 'integrity'). Remember though, integrity is a structural phenomenon. It's not a moral issue so much as a matter of clear insight into the way the universe operates. If we neglect to acknowledge the spiritual dimension in ourselves, then we'll be forced to rely on the scarcity-based mind to guide our actions. If our actions stem from the level of mind, our communications will be inauthentic and our audience's spiritual filter will stay shut. The logic of this process is flawless: sent messages always resonate with the receiver on the same existential level from which they originated. We call this principle the "law of resonance."

How are we to know from what existential level our messages are being sent? First off, look at your audience. Are they disinterested? If so, there's a good chance that you are being inauthentic. Authenticity can be clearly observed through it's joyful reflection in the eyes of our listeners. Granted, in many communication design situations we do not have a live person or audience right in front of us. How are we then to know? We must be willing to check our ego and take a clear-eyed look at our intentions. Authenticity has everything to do with intentions, and intentions are almost always hidden—especially from ourselves.

In any situation, the easiest way to determine if you are being authentic is to ask yourself: Is my true intention in this situation to give or to get? It's that simple. If your intention is to give, without expectations, this means that you have identified yourself as someone with infinite supply, or abundance. You have chosen to trust in the invisible supply. You are being authentic. If your intention is to get (or trade) something, this means that you have identified yourself as someone with limited amount, or scarcity. You have chosen to trust primarily in the visible universe. You may be acting like a smart scientist or business person, but you are denying the source. You are being inauthentic. The choice is yours. But only giving demonstrates and engenders trust.

To maintain authenticity, we must train ourselves to remember that the true source of life is beyond the senses. We must cultivate deep faith in this source, and be humble enough to let it operate through us as often as possible. As we do this, we'll start to see powerful results in our communications with others—results that undo our skepticism and justify our faith. Eventually we'll see that fear and manipulation are neither bad nor good, they're just a bit depressing. They demonstrate that we have lost touch with our own nature.

Inspiration is the remembrance of the vitality of nonsense—a mode of experiencing life that literally transcends the senses. It is the best teacher this world has ever known, because it comes from an unimaginably fertile and prolific ground beyond this chaotic realm of shifting forms. A fleeting taste of the truth can erase years of confusion and doubt. If you'd like to create and deliver messages that have this impact on others, your first goal must be to develop a heartfelt commitment to always getting clear about your underlying intentions, and to observing what these intentions appear to indicate about who you think you are.

2) The Principle of Context

Sometimes authenticity needs strategic help. Because most adults have accumulated years of baggage, they can be quite stubborn and unwilling to trust anyone, authentic or not. As inspirational communicators, we must be prepared to deal with the mental resistance that cynicism creates. We must understand how to strategically present information to increase the likelihood that our listeners will loosen their grip on their self-protective minds. This requires a deep grasp of context.

The principle of context proposes that all human minds operate out of hidden themes or assumptions about what the purpose of human life is. These core assumptions can be boiled down to a simple life-theme statement such as, "The purpose of life is to prove oneself worthy to enter heaven," or "The purpose of life is to sacrifice our own wants now, for the betterment of all mankind." Believe it or not, simple statements like this create an invisible context, like a bowl, in which all of our thoughts occur. Core values, resonant metaphors, occupational choices, favorite hobbies, mate preferences—all of these derive their purpose and meaning within this hidden set of assumptions. We can't see them; we see *with* them.

Inspirational communicators instinctively sense the deep hidden contexts that their audiences carry around with them, and have the rare ability to help these audiences escape the pernicious limitations that these unconscious contexts impose. What a gift to offer a person! When someone can suddenly see that their entire worldview has been unnecessarily constrained by their thoughts, they feel a tremendous surge of freedom. They spontaneously experience their 'self' as the unconditional maker of the context (spirit) rather than the context itself (the mind). This is the metaphysical explanation for bliss and all so-called 'peak' experiences.

Assuming authentic intentions, the secret to accomplishing this magical effect is to use words, sounds, and symbols in a way that inspires our audience to question the validity of pre-existing assumptions they hold about the world. The second step is to use these same tools to help them imagine the possibility of a new, more expansive context. This process can be as dramatic or as silly as we choose to make it. One of the most pleasant ways to undo an outdated, limiting context is with humor.

Comedians understand the principle of context very well. A great comedian inhabits a space right behind the mind and is constantly using tricky thoughts to create and destroy contexts, leaving the audience laugh-stricken and speechless. The best laughs are always at our own expense, when we spontaneously see how absurd and pointless our beliefs can really be. By contrast, have you ever seen a bad comedian? Is there anything more painful? Bad comedians are bad because they are trapped in their own mind (or context, "I need the approval of others to survive") and they are unable to get the existential leverage required to pull others out of their rigid mental orbits.

Besides humor, there are several other time-tested tactics that inspirational communicators can use to urge audiences to revisit their existing context and open their spiritual filter. Some major spiritual filter engaging tactics include: *listening, unspoken truths, demonstrating trust, repetition and rhyme, story payoffs, limiting metaphors, transformational metaphors, solutions, calls to duty, calls to action, calls to imagine* and *silence.*

LISTENING: Listening is the quickest way to get another person to open up to the shared spiritual dimension, and a cherished tool of all inspirational masters. When we listen, we pull for another to express and release all of the accumulated guilt lodged between their mind and spirit. In fact, listening is such a powerful and varied tool that it truly deserves a special communication manual of its own.

Why is listening so powerful? Because it directly employs the law of existential leveraging. In order to really listen, we must choose to identify with a deep level of self, which calls for a matching response in our audience. Put differently, our listening creates an unbounded context that promotes expanded experiential capacity, or space, in the speaker. Expanded experiential space is good, because it allows the listened-to person to spontaneously see through the muddy contents of the mind, to the core assumptions from which their thoughts are arising.

One big logistical limitation with regard to listening is that it is primarily limited to in-person social interactions. If we are designing communications for distribution through mass media (print, TV, radio, etc.), communication is still mostly a one-way street. In these situations, we must rely on our authenticity and skillful application of the rhetorical tools outlined below to achieve the same impact.

UNSPOKEN TRUTHS: In most 'civilized' communications we find ourselves tap-dancing around issues in order not to offend or upset people. Unconsciously, audiences often resent this politeness, experiencing it as a subtle signal of mistrust. If you want to earn trust quickly and effectively, one explosive tactic is to say the very thing that everyone else seems to be avoiding. Call out the proverbial elephant in the room. Some people may be shocked, some may be offended—but

Inspiration in Action #7: Charismatic leadership for dummies

"Ask not what your country can do for you, but what you can do for your country"—John F. Kennedy was a one of the most inspiring leaders in American history. Would you like to know the biggest secret behind his transformational charisma? Here goes: JFK called upon Americans to view their patriotism through the lens of service, or contribution. True contribution always inspires the giver, because it causes them to see themselves from a perspective of strength. Taking, conversely, can cause people to see themselves as weak and needy. It's a secret mental dynamic that all transformational leaders intuitively employ.

many will be grateful, especially if you do so gracefully. In telling the truth you have helped liberate them from the suffocating influences of the 'cultured' comfort-seeking mind. Effectively stating unspoken truths requires a special combination of courage and tact, and gets easier with practice and/or a few alcoholic beverages.

DEMONSTRATING TRUST: This one is simple, but potent. Showing others that you trust them instinctively calls upon them to trust you in kind. In a society littered with law firms and security systems, strangers have grown sadly unaccustomed to being treated with genuine trust. Trust others without explanation and you will evoke a sense of openness, warmth and connection in even the toughest of audiences.

REPETITION AND RHYME: Don't underestimate the raw evocative power of sound, especially when formed into pleasing patterns and textures intended to deliver an emotionally resonant message. Repetition and rhyme have an uncanny ability to draw listeners away from an analytical mode of processing and into a more aesthetic beauty-driven mode. Physiologically speaking, such sounds relax the brain and pull the listener into what scientists call an "alpha state" (characterized by enhanced receptiveness and suggestibility).

Embracing this principle, great communicators throughout time —particularly great orators, poets and hypnotists—have invariably sprinkled repetition and rhyme liberally throughout their works. Doing so gives one's communications the same powerful, trance-inducing quality of music, and gently relaxes the spiritual filter.

STORY PAYOFFS: Story payoffs are to inspiration what orgasms are to procreation. The true power of stories comes not from their capacity to entertain audiences (read: open mental filters), but from their ability to vicariously transform audiences (read: open spiritual filters). A well-told story is an inspired context delivery vehicle that discreetly conveys a certain theme—or context—to the listener. Ideally, this theme will be embedded throughout the story,

Inspiration in Action #8: Red pill or blue pill?

Poets, philosophers and mystics have long observed that most humans live in a world of unnecessary scarcity and limitation. For example, Plato's infamous "Cave Allegory" likened most people to cave dwellers unaware that the world they see is but the flicker of shadows on a wall. A similar metaphor was used in the 1999 blockbuster "The Matrix." In this movie, when the main character Neo is forced to choose between the world of voluntary delusion (blue pill) and the world of uncompromising truth (red pill), he chooses truth… an inspiring choice, and an inspired metaphor that launched a ridiculously successful movie franchise. Times and fashions may change—truth doesn't.

and only become clear upon the story's final climax, or payoff.

A well-told story delivers its theme in an emotionally resonant way, avoiding dry intellectual analysis. As a result, audiences do not feel manipulated; they feel inspired. Why do you think the major religions have lasted for so long? Because all major religions are propagated through gripping stories with hugely thematic and resonant payoffs. If you want to truly inspire an audience, embed your message into the climax of a great story. Who knows? Maybe someday you'll get good enough to start your own cult.

SOLUTIONS: Solutions are to problems what story payoffs are to stories. If you have first done a good job using questions to develop the awareness of an explicit need or problem in your audience, you must then offer a clear solution. Doing so will inspire them. Why? Because solutions symbolically represent safety and security. These feelings create in our audience a context of gratitude and a willingness to let go of self-protecting, survival-based thinking.

LIMITING METAPHORS: A great way to loosen someone's grasp on their current world view is to ask them to consider the negative or limiting impact that their current preferred metaphors may be having on their life. For example, if someone views life as a brutal game, we might ask them to consider what toll brutal gamesmanship may be exacting upon their close personal relationships. All metaphors serve a helpful function, but also carry with them insidious limitations. If you can get an audience to consider these limitations, you will create space and willingness for new insights to emerge.

TRANSFORMATIONAL METAPHORS: This involves inviting our audience to consider replacing their limiting life metaphors with less limiting, more expansive ones. For example if someone views the world as a *battle* to survive, we might encourage them to consider looking at life as a *test* that they must pass. A test requires discipline and promises a future payoff. Such a metaphor will help instill the person with a sense of security and a greater capacity to delay gratification. Alternatively, if a person views life as a test that they must pass, we might encourage them to view the world as a *game* they can win. This may help them release their fear of authority and engage fuller self-expression.

Transformational metaphors give people a new, more expansive way of framing their most pressing life challenges. But, to be effective, transformational metaphors must be selected based upon a clear understanding of the limitations of the organizing metaphors your audience is currently using. We'll spell out the precise transformational metaphors to use depending upon your audience in later chapters.

CALL TO DUTY: A traditional favorite technique for religious and nationalistic initiatives, the "call to duty" is a tactic that can be used to inspire audiences to adopt a sacrificial mental context in which they passionately embrace an opportunity to contribute as part of a larger social movement. This often works well with people who feel isolated and who seek a larger life-purpose, and can be used for positive social initiatives of any stripe—political, economic, environmental, spiritual, etc.

CALL TO ACTION: A favorite technique for sports and corporate sales initiatives, the "call to action" can be used to inspire audiences to adopt an expressive context in which they overcome inertia and create tangible real-world results. This can work wonders with people who feel timid, shy, or unmotivated, but can be used to energize any audience.

CALL TO IMAGINE: A favorite technique of (and for) creatives, the "call to imagine" is a profound way to inspire audiences to engage their mental faculties towards the creation of an inspired future vision. This works for anyone willing to discard cynicism and let their imagination flow. The proposed future context, if believed, will mobilize the power of dreams towards the advancement of life-serving goals.

SILENCE: Sometimes the best way to invite inspiration is with empty space. Great communicators often leave pregnant pauses in their messages, giving their words, sounds and visual images time to resonate on a transcendent level. Silent space naturally brings an aura of presence, because it allows listeners to observe (and quiet) the ramblings of their own noisy minds. When the mind becomes observed as 'other,' audiences shift towards identification with the silent background behind all thought. When all is said and done, mental silence is the creative ground from which all inspiration must ultimately emerge.

So there you have it—a laundry list of proven spiritual filter-overcoming techniques. At the end of the day, each of these techniques will be only as inspirational as the communicator is authentic. But, artfully employed

---

Inspiration in Action #9: Trusting for dollars

In 2007, alternative rock group Radiohead infuriated the mainstream music industry establishment by offering their newly released album exclusively online with a 'pay what you want' pricing strategy. Free-market fundamentalists and keepers of the old-school music distribution outlets quickly predicted disaster and doom. But Radiohead's profitability and fanbase have only increased. Why did this approach work so well? Because people are inherently trustworthy and appreciate being trusted, of course! Since this time, other prominent acts have followed suit, much to the music industry's chagrin.

Filter	Design Goal	Engagement Tactics
Sensory (WHAT)	Capture Attention	surprise, aesthetics, sensory design (visual, auditory, kinesthetic, etc.), media type, media placement
Mental (HOW)	Generate Interest	situation framing, personal recognition, value framing, questioning, problem making, storytelling, resonant metaphors
Spiritual (WHY)	Transcend Thinking	authenticity, humor, listening, unspoken truths, demonstrating trust, repetition and rhyme, story payoffs, solutions, limiting metaphors, transformational metaphors, calls to duty, calls to action, calls to imagine, silence

with a true intention to serve, these tactics will unlock your audience's spiritual energies and help them break free from the suffocating influence that obsessive thinking causes. For a quick summary of all of these engagement tactics and the design goals that each is meant to serve, please refer to the summary table above.

The irony of inspiration

Here's the rub: people crave inspiration, but they usually fight like hell when we try to inspire them. Why? Because they sense a bunch of gunk and goo between themselves and their spirit. They intuit that, in order to get the grand prize of happiness, they'll have to weather the storm of repressed guilt that they've been pushing aside for so long. A great communicator understands this dynamic and employs the tactics we've covered to create a context of hope in which people are finally willing to let this guard down and stop running from fearful shadows in their minds.

You've probably heard the true stories of prison inmates who, upon being released from a long incarceration, promptly commit a random crime in order to regain access to the prison from where they came. This is a true phenomenon—it happens all the time. From the outside this behavior seems so bizarre. Why would someone willingly choose to give up their freedom to live in cramped squalor? The answer is simple: they lack faith in the unknown. They prefer the hell they know to the one they don't know. This is how almost all humans are in relation to the cramped prisons they've constructed, or—if you prefer—their minds.

The only way to get a prisoner to enjoy freedom is to help them feel safe and point them in the right direction. Existentially speaking, this is what truly inspirational communicators do. With this thought in mind, please put the book down right now and go watch a speech by the great Martin Luther King, Jr. (visit www.thekingcenter.org). He was the living embodiment of the principles we're espousing. More than any other communicator I've studied, he was gifted at creating a safe context in which people were willing to confront and release mental shadows. But as great as he was, we all have this ability if we are humble enough, brave enough, and willing to do our homework.

What is the spiritual filter...really?

When it comes right down to it, the spiritual filter is actually a survival strategy invented by the mind to keep us from pain and suffering. It is a storage device for all the past pain we once judged as purposeless. After a few decades of living, most of us accumulate many such experiences, and our spiritual filter grows thick and impenetrable. This mass of undigested pain was termed "the shadow" by psychologist Carl Jung. According to Jung's judgement this shadow is always "ninety-nine percent pure gold" for the individual who has the courage to confront it. This is because it is only by confronting and transcending the shadow that we can regain access to the spiritual energies that sustain us.

The only power a shadow can have is the power we give it by refusing to look at it. The root of refusal is always fear, which is the polar opposite of inspiration. Fears come in many forms, but they always stem from one primary cause: our belief in the notion of *separateness*.

Think about it. Fear couldn't exist without an observing consciousness that believes itself separate from everything else and in danger. The idea of separation entered our minds at a very early age and caused us to seek safety. This seeking became a deeply ingrained mental habit, and grew into a whole host of other mental habits naively intended to protect us. Ultimately, in the name of safety, we have developed an insatiable need for approval from others and a strong urge to control our environment.

This is how our mental machinery works. These three primary motives—safety, approval, and control—are the building blocks of all mental activity.[4] Without them we probably wouldn't even have occasion to think. Consider this: what would your mind do if you felt completely safe, loved, and in control? Nothing. Your mind would either disappear in a puff of smoke, or invent some new problem to fret about! That's what the mind does—it creates and solves problems. Period.

When we dig down to the very core, we'll discover that all of our safety-seeking is held in place by the insane notion that we are each hopelessly separated from the source of life. And, if we take this flawed idea as fact, then we naturally begin to view the world as a vicious fight to maximize pleasure and minimize pain. So what are we to do with pain as it arises in the course of living? We learn to stuff it away at a deeper level of mind. Over time, this is how we lose our passion for living. In Transformational Design jargon, this is how our "spiritual filter" gets "clogged."

"The only thing we have to fear is fear itself"...Roosevelt was an inspiring fellow. He understood that to experience inspiration one must be fearless and resolute towards the shadow, because without fear the shadow couldn't even exist! Light easily destroys all shadows, because shadows can only exist in spaces without light. It's an existential riddle. Get it?

The key to inspiring others is not to become a shadow-boxer, but to somehow call into question the flawed idea that led to our creating the shadow in the first place: the notion that we are fundamentally separate from each other and from life's source. From the vantage point of the senses, only the body is real and the inspiration is smoke and mirrors. From the vantage point of spirit, inspiration is real and life in the physical body is "a tale told by an idiot, full of sound and fury, signifying nothing."[5] Both perspectives can be argued—but which do you prefer?

Inspiration in Action #10: Did MLK read this book?

Martin Luther King's legendary "I Have a Dream" speech will go down as one of the most pivotal moments in U.S. history. King's eloquent words stand the test of time not just because of his passion and authenticity, but also because he was a brilliant rhetorical tactician. In almost every recorded speech he strategically employed communication tactics to overcome resistance in his listeners and engage the spiritual filter. In this particularly famous speech he used the rhythmic repetition of a transformational metaphor (embedded in the phrase "I have a dream") to open audience receptivity for a passionate call to imagine a world without racism. Worked pretty well, yes?

If you want to inspire others, choose to have faith in your connection to the source of life, and in the unity behind appearances. The results you generate will more than justify your faith. Plus, it's much more fun.

Creating "bottom of soul" awareness

Branding and marketing gurus have long spoken fondly of "top of mind awareness." With the current approach, we seek to create something much better: bottom of soul awareness. The mind is the province of persuasion, but the soul is the gateway to transformation. To design media and communications with this kind of soul resonance, we must be willing to swim out past the shallow waters and meet our audience in the deep end. This requires a practical understanding of the three filters and how to engage them, but it also requires a willingness to explore the role that our intentions play in the communication design process.

As you may have noticed, the vast majority of mass media marketing initiatives stop well short of inspiration, seeking instead to persuade or manipulate. In fact, in practice, most advertising professionals spend the lion's share of their creative energies focusing on the shallowest possible dimension: the sensory. Endless discussions about media type, design style, and ad placement fill the days at large and small firms alike, with little or no dialogue regarding the spiritual implications of the approach.

Question: Why do we have an industry of brilliant and talented people who are so ill-equipped to grasp the spiritual dynamics of the communication process?

Answer: Outdated maps!

Until now, we've lacked a clear language and clear practical model for understanding how to systematically access these deeper layers of a human (bio-psycho-social) being. In the absence of a lucid, practical model, all we had to go on is what we could see, touch, taste, hear, smell, and intuit by the sweat of our brow. But now we finally have a clear model. It compensates for the gaps left by earlier models without invalidating any of them. It gives us a simple framework for solving complex communication problems that we could always vaguely feel in our gut, but could never quite articulate.

Inspiration in Action #11: The power of small thinking

In 1959, NY advertising firm DDB created an automotive marketing initiative that consistently ranks as the best ad campaign of all time. Titled "Think Small," this campaign successfully launched the eccentric 'new' Volkswagon Beetle using communication tactics that defied all conventions: It downplayed the VW brand, challenged consumers to alter their mindset, and ultimately even mocked their own product by calling it a 'lemon'. From a Transformational Design perspective, the reason for this campaign's success is abundantly clear: it instantly captured the viewers' senses by defying expectations, and then seamlessly delivered an authentic and perspective-shifting call to imagine.

CHAPTER 04

·····

INSPIRATION CAUSES TRANSFORMATION

·····

"Wanna make the world a better place? Fix yourself, then there'll be one less scoundrel among us."
- Thomas Carlyle (paraphrase)

This book is called "Igniting Inspiration," not "Igniting Transformation." But over time these concepts amount to the exact same thing. All transformations are inspired, and all inspiration causes transformation, however hidden. In this chapter we will examine the ever-chic concept of transformation through our nifty new lens, and also explore some practical implications for those of us who are audacious enough to actively seek transformative experiences for ourselves and others.

Three types of transformation

Simply defined, a 'transformation' is a change in form. Given our dimensional perspective, there are three distinct orders, or degrees, of transformation that may occur on two or more dimensions (material and mental) as follows:

PHYSICAL TRANSFORMATION
Measurable change in a person's body, physical environment, or life situation. Familiar examples include dramatic weight loss, financial breakthroughs, and plastic surgery. Physical transformations are leveraged using energies from the mental sphere, and are only sustainable when they derive from fundamental shifts in thinking.

MENTAL TRANSFORMATION
Change in mental orientation (attitudes, beliefs, etc.) towards certain topics and objects. Familiar examples include a positive change in attitude towards one's job or spouse, shifts in political ideology and/ or a generally enhanced sense of motivation and well-being. Mental

transformations precede any sustainable physical transformation, and are accompanied by a slight-to-moderate reshaping of the spiritual filter (i.e., release of guilt and shame, forgiveness of past hurts, emotional purging and catharsis).

Spiritual Transformation

A permanent shift in the way one experiences the world. Usually correlated with a dramatic change in one's core values and spontaneous alterations in long-established life habits. Familiar examples include dramatic religious conversions, unexplained physical healings, midlife crises, and spiritual awakenings caused by near death experiences. Spiritual transformations are leveraged through direct personal encounter and unconditional surrender to spiritual energies, allowing one's worldview to be fundamentally purged and reconstituted.

The take-home message? All transformations are not created equal. Any sustainable change to the human system (physical, mental or spiritual) must ultimately be leveraged from the highest level, or spirit, but there is tremendous variance in terms of intensity and duration. Spiritual transformations produce effects that ripple down through the entire bio-psycho-social system and are by far the most long-lasting. But they are also the most mysterious and the most difficult to achieve.

The cycle of spiritual transformations

If we hope to inspire spiritual transformations in others, we must understand the cyclical dynamics through which they occur. We must also grasp the awesome level of faith and courage that a person must posses in order to willingly allow such a life-changing inner process to unfold.

Spiritual transformations require a person to surrender the very context, or existential framework, that they are currently using to make sense of the world. This is akin to opening Pandora's Box. All of the ghosts and goblins of one's guilt-ridden past comes rushing headlong to be confronted and released. Why would anyone choose to do such a crazy thing? Doubt, of course. Profound existential doubt.

Spiritual transformations unravel when we begin to seriously doubt the validity of our most deeply held beliefs about ourselves. When this doubt becomes too intense, we lose our existential footing and disidentify with our habitual mental constructs. Often after a period of deep discomfort and a cathartic emotional purging, we experience a deep sense of freedom and a liberating expansion of mental/experiential space. The fear that had kept us imprisoned disappears, because it was merely a by-product of limiting beliefs that we have since surrendered.

It's ironic to realize that the actual killer is always the mind's unchecked *fear* of a killer. The mind is a charlatan, a wing-nut, a hack. It tries to convince us that we won't be safe without its sage guidance, but it is mistaken. In truth, the mind is properly used as a tool to serve the spirit, and is pathetically ill-equipped to serve as master for any life domain. It has no internal compass! When we finally stop buying into our own mental chatter, our agony transforms into laughter. We realize that the joke was on us. The birds start to sing again, and life is great for a little while—until the transformational cycle begins anew. Until we make another rigid belief system. Until life calls us into another dark night.

There's no way around it. Nature moves in circles—the sun, the moon, seasons, and human emotions. But there is some good news here: eventually a person grows to accept and even *enjoy* this process. Eventually, after undergoing enough of these cycles, one starts to understand that this powerful ebb and flow of spiritual energies is how life operates. This cycle is to be celebrated, not feared. Who are we to say it should be any different? What do we know? At this stage of thinking, instead of avoiding transformation, a person begins to actively seek and even revel in it.

At this advanced stage, one begins to experience life as a fluid dance where forms, seen and unseen, emerge and dissipate ever upward and onward. This person starts to experience an overwhelming sense of gratitude for the pure, unbridled joy of being. Through clarity and insight, they develop an almost magical ability to tap into the vital energies of other human beings and lift them up the ladder of human existence. Why is this important to know in a book on inspirational communication? Because it is here that a human becomes instinctively and profoundly inspirational.

In the end, experiencing this joyful state of being is my wish for everyone reading this book, that your capacity to inspire others will grow naturally from your gratitude for being alive, and from your intrinsic desire to express this joyful feeling to others.

What changes do you want to see?

If you had your wish, what change in the world would you most want to make? Would you rid the world of nuclear weapons and gas-guzzling cars? Save the polar bears? End racism? Cause world peace? Whatever it is, if you look closely enough, you'll see that the changes you're after are material symbols for something beyond form—a subjective state of being. If we look deeply enough, we see that all of our noble intentions to change the world are built upon the hidden assumption that somehow by doing this we'll attain a lasting personal sense of fulfillment and peace. It's never about the world—it's always about *us*.

Is this such a bad thing? Should we be ashamed and embarrassed? Nope. It's the human condition. But once we admit this to ourselves and start to examine the world through this symbolic lens, we notice something

---

Inspiration in Action #12: How an old fogey inspired millions

In 1988, journalist Bill Moyers sat down with mythology expert Joseph Campbell to discuss mankind's oldest stories, or myths. The resulting PBS documentary (titled "The Power of Myth") became the most highly acclaimed series in PBS's history and launched an unprecedented resurgence in the study of world mythology. Why was this humble documentary so transformational? Because with authenticity and grace, Campbell showed how personally relevant these ancient stories are for us today. He spent his entire life delivering this simple, inspired message. With his landmark book "A Hero with a Thousand Faces" he also inspired George Lucas to invent the original Star Wars trilogy. Don't you wish Lucas had revisited Campbell before filming the final three?

peculiar: with all of our bickering and power struggles we humans all have exactly the same underlying goal. We want to be happy. Period. End of story. The infinity of forms that this shared goal can take is staggeringly complex, but the underlying subtext is always quite simple. All seeking, without exception, is meant to take us to the inner utopia of unbridled joy. This is the only goal that any human being has ever truly sought.

Once we accept that our material goal is but a symbol, we experience ourselves—and our species—as the butt of a tremendous cosmic joke of our own making. We've been seeking in the external world for something that doesn't even exist: inner peace. Furthermore, all seeking, no matter how noble, serves merely to mask this truth. In fact, most of our seemingly 'noble' seeking is secretly guided by a not-so-noble quest to be and/or appear morally superior. We have unconsciously concluded that happiness would consist in our 'specialness' and superiority, and we have cleverly hid this quest from ourselves by dressing our intentions up in the sunshine-happy spin of altruistic jargon.

Here's the bottom-line: seeking to improve the world is a futile game built upon a lie. The sooner we realize this and release our misguided agenda, the sooner we can become a reflection for that part of us beyond all agendas. And when we start to reflect this type of awesome energy, we are effortlessly authentic and inspiring. We radiate with a sense of possibility that automatically reminds everyone around us of their own unbounded, spiritual nature. Most people don't yet have a mental framework for understanding this process, but everyone instinctively gets it. The hidden truth that all great communicators understand is that we don't inspire people by trying to make them better, we inspire them by witnessing their inherent perfection.

Perhaps the ultimate irony of existence is that the people who actually do ignite massive spiritual transformations in this world are the ones who have given up seeking altogether. Sure, they often play the games of form. They have jobs, raise children, pay taxes, deliver speeches, and sometimes even cause a major ruckus in the middle of town square, but they have detached from the whole material world in a fundamental way. Through inspiration itself, they have come to see that to overly identify with material forms is to lose access to the underlying source, and to relinquish existential leverage.

So what now?

Please don't mistake this argument for disrespect, or my words for truth. Truth is beyond words, beyond emotions, beyond all of this mind-made stuff. What we're doing here is using words, or symbols, to point towards a spiritual truth beyond all words. To take our learning from the realm of intellect into the realm of direct experience, we must be willing to expose the arrogant 'do-gooder' spiritual filter that would have us believe that changing the world is a valuable purpose for living.

Why do we need a purpose for living when living is life's purpose? What could possibly be more important than life? Until we choose to remember that life is the only legitimate purpose, we will create neither sustainable communications nor sustainable solutions to the myriad self-imposed problems of our world. Instead, we will rely on dead, duct tape solutions lead by the twin mind-demons of dry logic and dogma.

Belief is irrelevant when we have clarity and faith in our convictions. And, ultimately, conviction is what inspires. We must tolerate no self-deception if we aim to be the kind of human who can pull others to greatness. I'm assuming that you are that brave, uncommonly truthful sort of person or you wouldn't be reading this book.

When we are willing to let the light shine through our spiritualized ego, we develop a profound new vision, a sort of spiritual X-ray. We begin to observe how it is in fact our hidden lack of authenticity that attracts every new situation to us as a fresh opportunity to release unwanted guilt and embrace a deeper truth. We also see that this process is the hidden purpose of life, and is never-ending in ourselves and in everyone we meet. Most importantly for present purposes, we see that "communication" is just a five-syllable word that we use to represent the amazingly orchestrated process through which life's relentless push towards realization expresses itself between us humans. Inspiration is the fuel, and transformation is its never-ending footprint.

CHAPTER 05

.....

TEN UNIVERSAL PRINCIPLES OF INSPIRATION

.....

1. *Inspiration is our natural state but we are usually unaware of it.*

2. *Lies kill inspiration. Truth ignites it.*

3. *Inspiration originates from neither the body nor the mind. It arises from a deeper dimension than perception.*

4. *A message's authenticity and perceived personal relevance are the two critical factors that determine its inspirational potency.*

5. *Inspiration cannot be forced. The best one can do is create proper conditions by being authentic and by strategically removing barriers to its emergence.*

6. *Inspired actions are intrinsically enjoyable, breeding repetition and a sense of ownership. All sustainable behaviors derive from inspiration (rather than from force or persuasion).*

7. *Inspiration must ultimately lead to measurable real-world results or it will backfire, over time, creating a deepened sense of cynicism and resignation.*

8. *A sender's own intentions infuse the message with a quality that calls for a similar matching frequency in the receiver. This is the law of resonance.*

9. *When the guiding intention behind a message stems from the sender's identification with self as source (spiritual dimension) rather than outcome (body and mind), the receiver will generally perceive the message as authentic.*

10. *Sustained inspiration adds constant creative energy to a person's mental system, which ultimately produces a wholesale transformation of their worldview. This process is the ongoing basis for mankind's mental and spiritual evolution on both a micro (personal) and macro (global) level.*

Part II.

THE DIFFERENCES: How do people differ meaningfully?

In Part II we'll destroy the "People-Are" fallacy once and for all. We'll explore some exciting scientific research that shows how people mentally evolve over time as they confront and resolve a somewhat predictable set of core existential dilemmas. We'll also explore how a person's state of mental complexity influences the way they look at the world. This will help us frame messages in a way that resonates with people of all backgrounds.

← "HOW" IS HERE

CHAPTER 06

. . . . .

ENTERING THE REAL WORLD

. . . . .

`"Can't we all just get along?" - Rodney King`

Soaring rhetoric about spiritual unity is one thing. Getting people to play nice together is another. All idealists learn sooner or later that good intentions have a very short shelf-life in a society built for profit and speed. Separation may not be real in the ultimate sense, but it certainly seems real to our five senses. Our eyeballs show us a world of minds and bodies struggling for power, bickering over everything under the sun.

Some people believe that taxes are killing our economy; others believe that tax loopholes are doing it. Some people worry that we are destroying the planet's delicate ecosystems with reckless commerce; others worry that we are destroying our commerce with reckless environmentalism. Some people think bombing is an effective way to deter those who hate us; others think that bombing creates legions of new haters.

Darwin defined two species as "speciated" when they became so genetically dissimilar that they could no longer procreate to make babies. It appears that a similar thing is happening on a mental level with us today, something I call "speciation of consciousness." Our minds have grown so dissimilar that we can hardly communicate to make the babies (aka "solutions") to the most basic problems of living.

If we really want to have an impact on this world, we've got to stop preaching to the converted and start learning how to inspire conversions in the uninitiated. The mind is a filter for personal relevance; it is the thuggish bodyguard that keeps inspiration out. In order to get the mind to bow down to the call of inspiration, we must first engage it on its own turf—the values and schemas that it deeply cherishes. That is the true leadership challenge of our time. Not to persuade, but to engage deeply so that we might all collectively surrender to something larger—a shared purpose in the service of our one shared life.

A new train is coming

Fortunately life is infinitely adaptive and resilient. At the expanding margins of our culture we now see emerging a new way of thinking that offers remedy to the self-righteousness and mental gridlock that have kept us enslaved. It is a more systemic, less ideological way of engaging the world that manages to grasp the hidden simplicity behind the overwhelming myriad of meanings in our culture, as well as the emergent complexity that simple solutions can create. We see this new thinking system expressing itself most clearly in advanced strains of the environmental, progressive, and LOHAS ("lifestyle of health and sustainability") movements, but it cannot be defined by any one of these. Like fresh sprouts from a long-buried seed, these movements are saplings from the deeper soil of our collective awareness.

This new way of looking at the world is an evolution unseen in the recorded history of mankind. From the ground up, it is helping us to resolve the mental blockages that have kept us entangled because it has learned to embrace all of the old ways of looking at the world without getting bogged down by any of them. It shines fresh light and creates insights where before there was only confusion and disdain. This new thinking system is our greatest tool for creating new, inspired communication systems and leadership platforms that can move us out of collective global deadlock and towards a future where hope is celebrated.

The book you're holding was written *from* this new level of thinking *for* this new level of thinking. The Transformational Design™ model is actually just a well-articulated conceptual demonstration of this new thinking system in action—but there are many others, and they are cropping up in every nook and cranny of our economic, political and cultural landscape. This wave is bigger than all of us, smarter than all of us, and it's spreading fast through us. By the end of Section II, you'll know exactly what this new thinking system looks like and how it operates. In fact, you'll soon be consciously applying this new thinking system (or 'map') to diagnose and unclog your fellow beings' existential blockages to help them regain access to that renewable source of energy that is their inner inheritance. Functionally speaking, this is what inspirational leaders do. Through inspiration, communication and leadership become one.

Inspiration in Action #13: The unifying power of vision

On May 25, 1961 John F. Kennedy gave a speech that energized America to push the boundaries of human accomplishment by sending the first human to the moon. At the time, the cold war was freezing and major domestic conflicts were festering. Skeptics laughed and cynics scorned, but eight years and $9 billion later the first manned moon mission landed. Kennedy was killed shortly after his speech, but his bold, inspiring vision remained. Here's a question for all of you modern-day visionaries to ponder: What do you imagine our next unifying American vision might be?

Looking forward

In order to accomplish our agenda, we will first outline some ground-breaking psychological research that spells out the precise developmental stages through which our minds evolve as we ascend the ladder of mental complexity. Then, we'll outline specific ways that we can integrate this new developmental research into our communication design process in order to consistently craft communications that inspire.

CHAPTER 07

.....

A MAP OF MENTAL COMPLEXITY

.....

"Everything should be made as simple as possible, but not simpler." - Albert Einstein

For years I consulted with clients armed with just the information we've covered so far—the three-dimensional model, tactics for overcoming the three filters, and a strong understanding of the dynamics of mental transformation. The results were usually quite good. My clients were happy, but I wasn't. This grand puzzle was still somehow missing a piece.

The problem was always with the mind. In practice, designing transformational communications boils down to overcoming the audience's mental and spiritual filters. Just conceptualizing that such filters exist was a big breakthrough, but it didn't give me enough practical information to go on. To be complete the model needed some solid scientific legs that could help me predict differences in the way the mental and spiritual filters operated across complex audiences over time. In short, it needed a scientifically tested, developmental map.

Psychologists have long sought to create such maps. Erik Erikson, Robert Kegan, Jean Piaget, Lawrence Kohlberg—all were brilliant psychologists and thinkers with wonderful insights. But none of their theories seemed to fit with the dimensional framework I'd fashioned. The model called for research that could somehow take into account the complex, dynamic nature of adult psychological development, yet still be easily applicable to everyday challenges.

I looked and looked. Eventually I stopped looking and entered into a sort of professional/existential early mid-life crisis. I gave up theorizing, stopped writing, and took a job as a traveling speaker for a national seminar company. It paid well, but it wasn't my calling. I'd given up on my calling. Who was I kidding? A practical metaphysical model of human leadership and communication?! Perhaps it was time to finally grow up...

And then it happened. One evening before a seminar outside a sleepy town in northern California, I got a call from an excited colleague who felt compelled to inform me about a book he was reading titled *Spiral Dynamics: Mastering Leadership, Values and Change.* I'd never heard of it. It was about a little-known theory of adult development based upon the work of a deceased psychologist who had somehow slipped under my graduate school radar. His name is Clare W. Graves. As fate would have it, I'd just been handed the final clue to this life-long query.

Enter Clare W. Graves

Psychologist Clare W. Graves developed an approach to human development that transcends all that came before or since. A humble professor and researcher during the 1950's and 60's, Graves attained only moderate popularity during his lifetime. And what a shame—because Graves's research is of earth-shaking significance for anyone interested in understanding people and collaborating to solve the problems of human existence.

Graves called his theory the "emergent-cyclical double-helix model of adult bio-psycho-social development." This description is not as important for understanding his work, as it is for helping you to grasp why most people have never heard of him. As mind-blowing as his findings were, his style was too stodgy and academic for mass consumption. Throw into

---

Inspiration in Action #14: Two degrees of Nelson Mandela

When South African leader Nelson Mandela was released from prison, he instantly became a revered global figurehead for peace and leadership. But what most people don't realize is that Gravesian consultant Dr. Don Beck had quietly been consulting with South African governmental leaders for more than 18 years to help make this transition possible. Using Graves' research as a conceptual framework, Dr. Beck helped design a color-coded communication system for important South African stakeholders that helped them collaborate in the service of a common vision, ending apartheid without igniting a civil war.

---

* Please note that the present approach to understanding, articulating, and applying Graves research (Transformational Design®) is fundamentally distinct from that used in Spiral Dynamics. Please see the 'Further Research' section for info on this and other Graves resources.

the mix the fact that his thinking was so far ahead of the curve, and you'll understand why his ideas never caught on, except with a select few highly advanced world leaders such as Nelson Mandela, Bill Clinton and Tony Blair, working behind the scenes with Gravesian consultants on global problems such as apartheid, immigration and international trade.

Until recently, Gravesian research and business applications have stayed mostly under the radar of mainstream awareness. Well, that time is over. The social, economic and environmental problems of our post-9/11 global society have left us with immense challenges that can only be solved by a framework of this scope and stature. In other words, the world is now ready for Graves. Expect to see much more of him in the years (and chapters) ahead.

The Gravesian framework

Graves viewed man's nature not as a set thing, but as an "ever emergent open system that evolves in saccadic quantum-like jumps."[6] He was particularly interested in understanding how a person's core values change as they evolve in complexity from one state to another. Unlike many researchers who focused on mental *disease*, he was interested in understanding mental *health* in its many forms. He observed that people have vastly different conceptions of what a healthy, mature adult is supposed to be. For decades he compiled a database of people's various conceptions of maturity. After decades of data collection and naturalistic behavioral observation, he discovered that there were actually only eight basic conceptions of a healthy human being operating in the world.

As he worked with these psychological conceptions, Graves discovered that they were far more than just aspirational ideals for psychological maturity. He discovered that, in fact, they represented eight fundamentally different ways of making sense of the world. Further, Graves proposed that each of us contains within our nervous system the potentiality of all eight thinking systems, spanning back to the first survival lessons of early man. These thinking systems represent distinct levels of human existence. They are as follows (see list on the next page):

LEVEL 1: *Autistic Thinking*
             (Date of Mass Origin: before 40,000 BCE)

LEVEL 2: *Magical/Tribal Thinking*
             (Date of Mass Origin: After 40,000 BCE)

LEVEL 3: *Heroic Thinking*
             (Date of Mass Origin: Approx. 8000 BCE)

LEVEL 4: *Absolutistic Thinking*
             (Date of Mass Origin: Approx. 4000–2000 BCE)

LEVEL 5: *Individualist Thinking*
             (Date of Mass Origin: Approx. 1300–1400 CE)

LEVEL 6: *Humanistic Thinking*
             (Date of Mass Origin: Approx. 1900 CE)

LEVEL 7: *Systemic Thinking*
             (Began Emerging Approx. 1950 CE)

LEVEL 8: *Holistic Thinking*
             (Origin in process)

According to Graves, each thinking system has emerged as an evolutionary adaptation of consciousness in response to survival challenges of a specific era. Using decades of data from an immense battery of psychological tests, discrete experimental observation, and common sense, he concluded that as a person progresses through each of these stages, she earns greater insight into the world and greater liberation from fear. He found that, over time, the mind of man vacillates between self-expression and self-sacrifice in a never ending upward spiral of emergent complexity.

Fancy, isn't it? Stick with me.

We will spend much time covering the specifics of these stages in the coming chapters, but to begin this life-changing educational process, we will start out simply—with a story. In the next few pages we'll take a didactic excursion through the dramatic narrative of mankind's psychological past, observing the evolution of our species through the Gravesian lens. As we pass through each stage of human development, take pause to consider how and when you might see these thinking systems showing up in our world still today. (*Quick note*: I've used the masculine 'he' for storytelling purposes, but this narrative is not gender specific.)

The spellbinding story of human emergence

LEVEL 1: *Autistic Thinking*

Like all animals, early man's main survival challenge was simply to eat, sleep and mate. Lacking a written language, religion, or a strong sense of self, this primal, preverbal human was probably driven almost completely by a need to satisfy immediate biological needs.

This simple drive-based approach to living continued unabated for untold thousands of years. Then something changed. Perhaps due to a major disruption to the earth's ecosystems or success in satisfying basic physiological urges, early man's mind developed a surplus of creative energy. A primitive notion of cause and effect entered his mind, and he started reaching out to fellow humans to create the first collaborative survival-based communities, or tribes.

BIRTH OF LEVEL 2: *Magical/Tribal Thinking*

This new tribal man lived in a mysterious world of magic and gods. Life and death, day and night passed in rhythmic succession, and he was but a helpless observer seeking the good graces of forces larger and much more powerful than himself. He was humble, fearful, and loyal. By observing the cycle of death and the events of nature, he sought to exert control over this world with religious rites and observances. Tribal leaders were the elders and shamans, those gifted with insights into the will of unseen, threatening gods. Others were left to follow the rites, rituals, and dictates handed down by tradition, to ensure the continued safety of the whole.

This primitive tribal culture worked, providing many enclaves of early humans with a level of security unmatched by their forefathers. However this success created the very conditions that felt suffocating to the spirit of the generations that followed. Having solved the most basic problems of living—food, shelter, protection—the curious, adventurous spirit of tribal man now surfaced. He began to question the value of living in fear of invisible gods and wondered what it might be like to explore life without all the sacrificial red tape and tribal restrictions.

Tribal man was becoming self-aware, an advancement that proved to be both a blessing and a curse. It blessed him with the promise of untold power and glory. It cursed him with the knowledge that he must destroy the old ways of living to achieve it. And so emerged a brazen new way of living, as the 'might-makes-right' ethic was born.

BIRTH OF LEVEL 3: *Heroic Thinking*
Finally unafraid to speak and act out in the pursuit of personal glory, heroic young adventurers set out to do battle, creating vast bloodthirsty empires and autocratic regimes. The old guard fought against it, but was helpless. This new consciousness was stronger, meaner and lawless.

Most failed on their heroic journeys. But some succeeded, building powerful empires where 'haves' ruled over the helpless 'have-nots.' These kingdoms lasted for thousands of years—sprawling kingdoms where the all-powerful few indulged in the finest things the world over, while the powerless many were left to slave in futility. Unlike earliest man, these beings were painfully aware of their own individuality. This awareness brought with it a sting of meaninglessness and a yearning for more. For the rich, the burning question was, "So what? With all of this power, I'm still just a human destined to die." For the masses, the sad realization was that their lives would never allow them the indulgences of kings: "Why me? What joy is to be found in this miserable life?" Rich and poor longed for something more than this world could offer. They wanted, finally, a sense of peace that couldn't be found in the realm of material wealth and worldly pleasure. Out of existential necessity, mankind had finally discovered and embraced the idea of one absolute God.

BIRTH OF LEVEL 4: *Absolutistic Thinking*

Within a short period, major monotheistic religions sprouted from every corner of the globe. Unlike previous nature-based religions, these religious systems promised more than mere protection from the forces of nature. They promised everlasting happiness and peace. The price: one must willingly sacrifice his enjoyment in the here-and-now. For most this was a fantastic bargain—the 'here-and-now' wasn't exactly a picnic anyway! At least now the poverty and powerlessness could be justified by a luxurious afterlife. Moral man began to find joy and purpose in the humble celebration of absolute truth, embodied in the image of heaven.

As the 'might-makes-right' ethic gave way to the more pious 'right vs. wrong' on a larger scale, dictatorial empires transformed into vast moralistic regimes based upon universal principles such as 'justice' and 'salvation' for the 'chosen people.' The obedient masses worked dutifully, spurring developments in agriculture and housing that raised the standard of living for everyone. It was an era of hard work, discipline and frugality. But, in the end, this newfound strength and piety did not bring the everlasting peace that humans were seeking. "Why must I wait until death to enjoy my life? What if this 'heaven' thing isn't true? Where's the proof?" Curiosity undermined their faith. The very safety and security that this saintly existence created led these humans to seek something beyond safety and security. Out of an ethic of self-sacrifice sprouted a new thinking style—bold, self-assertive and curious.

BIRTH OF LEVEL 5: *Individualistic Thinking*

Determined to shed the shackles of morality and enforced dogma, man became convinced that he could figure out how to understand and control the universe on his own merits. His agile mind generated endless questions. Old school religionists and moralists found these questions heretical. Struggles ensued and people were burned, but life continued and knowledge grew. Science was born. Philosophy prospered. Higher education proliferated. Soon the Renaissance had awakened, demonstrating man's divine ability to enact God's will on earth, as it is in heaven.

So began a time of unequalled prosperity and massive creativity. Financial empires began to accumulate in record numbers. Mechanical inventions allowed for massive production of goods and services. Transportation breakthroughs allowed these goods to be distributed throughout the planet. Possibility ruled the day. This process is still expanding today throughout the developing world, and for many (if not most) people worldwide, it represents the pinnacle of human aspiration.

But for others, material prosperity has come at too great a cost. A certain guilt and uneasiness has taken root. Improvement for improvement's sake has begun to ring hollow. Money and profit have lost their otherworldly glow. A simple, self-evident spiritual insight is begging for recognition: material wealth cannot offer inner peace. In a world of profit margins and bank mergers these disenchanted and soul-searching humans strive to de-emphasize materialism and turn towards the inward realm of feelings and relatedness with other human beings.

Birth of Level 6: *Humanistic Thinking*

Looking again at his soul, but without the black-and-white constraints of religious dogma, this human experiences the source of all life as the benevolent spirit of one's fellow man. It is the spirit of love, and it shows itself in a peace and kindness that transcends demographics. This human begins to value humanity for its own sake. A more complex form of religiosity emerges, one without the need of a hypothetical afterlife, or 'fire and brimstone' hell antics. Compassion and truth become the cherished antidotes to the poisons of victimization and capitalistic excess.

Spirit soars in the name of hope. This beautiful vision is pregnant with possibility—a utopian salvation seems right around the corner. We're all waiting...and yet nothing changes. Rent checks are still due. Credit cards still collect interest. Corporations still rape and pillage. Pollution escalates. Religious fanatics still plant pipe bombs in the name of 'truth.' Is this soaring philosophy just a nostalgic poem for the feel-good misfits? Romanticism falls upon the cold rocks of reality. Doubt poisons the love-fest.

Faced with the fact that nice guys finish last in a world of competitive global imperialism, many at this stage attempt to revert back to an earlier stage of self-indulgence. They become cynical, hardened, resigned. Others choose to bury their heads in the sand by diving headlong into the indulgences of spiritual excess. New age aphorisms and seminars keep their minds ever-charged with lofty notions not fit for the masses. But beyond regression to a soul-squelching past and hedonistic indulgence in an otherworldly now, lies a third option. The individual could surrender to the futility of seeking and renounce the game of survival.

For those with the gumption to surrender, a grand future awaits. The years spent looking inward have provided great training for the development of compassion. But, the problems of existence weren't solved. The person sees that the problems of existence are not merely caused by a lack of compassion, they are deeper and more systemic in nature. The problems of existence come from the very structures that mankind has created in order to attain safety and prosperity, and from his hidden delusions about his own nature. In order to solve these problems and give birth to a more prosperous humanity, this human now seeks to rethink all existing social structures and conventions, and redesign them so that they simultaneously serve mankind's physical, mental and spiritual needs...sustainably.

BIRTH OF LEVEL 7: *Systemic Thinking*
The person who makes it this far no longer buys into the notion that life is somehow an inherently scary ordeal. This person has begun to identify himself as the source of life itself, the same source that feeds every other life form in the universe. Gone are the days of idealistic 'live-and-let-live' thinking—the 'thrive-and-help-thrive' ethic has been born.

Humans at this stage are inspiring and uplifting problem-solvers with an almost magical insight into life. They are hearty leaders, capable of transcending divisive polemics in the effort to design workable social structures that bring people together in the service of life. They have reached the cutting-edge of popular consciousness and are riding an immense planetary wave. But the lessons are never done...

Although experts in the arts of creation and recreation, these folks still feel somehow once-removed from a more visceral connection with their own source. Eventually that timeless yearning in the human spirit once again pulls for something more, something beyond affluence with form. The soul longs to sacrifice itself again to a plane beyond this material world, beyond even the problem-solving systemic mind.

BIRTH OF LEVEL 8: *Holistic Thinking*
On the outermost fringes of our society today it appears that a new thinking system is yet being born. It is a holistic, intuitive thinking system well-grounded in the actualities of everyday living, but which has ceased to view them as fundamental to life itself. Instead, people who think this way seem to identify more with the unchanging spiritual essence of their being than with the ever-shifting world of forms.

The relatively few people who consistently embody this mindset are a joyful and peaceful lot. From the outside, they may seem mysterious and dreamy, but from the inside they are simply following the trusted guidance of their deeper selves. They are experiencing the long-forgotten truth about life that all of us will remember sooner or later: as humans, the essence of who we are is beyond knowing, beyond form, beyond the ravages of birth and death, beyond the opposites of love and hate. Life is an utter mystery. Only by fully embracing this mystery will we find lasting peace.

Now...take a deeeeep breath
This might be a good time to stand up, take a quick stretch and feed the cat. When you get back, we'll take a few minutes to review some implications that this story holds for those of us who are hell-bent on creating transformational media and communications.

Scaling the ladder of existence
As you read this narrative, it probably wasn't too difficult for you to relate to almost every single developmental stage along the way. This is because the relics of each and every stage exist in our minds right now, in our very physiological makeup. Graves believed that we have inherited

these thinking potentialities as part of the cellular DNA that directs our neuro-anatomical design. Common sense confirms this, as even the most enlightened individual doesn't have to look too deeply inside to find an inner caveman, tribesman, dictator, fundamentalist, capitalist, humanist, systems thinker and mystic just waiting to give their two cents.

As a communicator, you will find that knowing these eight thinking systems gives you unprecedented leverage for accessing audience inspiration, because each thinking system presupposes a certain habitual cognitive style for organizing and interpreting information. A person's mental and spiritual filters are the unconscious barriers that they must overcome to experience inspiration, and these filters are fundamentally shaped by the core values and assumptions of these eight meaning-making types.

Throughout this book we have defined an inspirational communicator as being a master of contexts—someone who can use words and symbols to create expanded new visions from which people can think and live. This Gravesian perspective makes this task much, much simpler. It spells out the eight fundamental contexts that a great communicator must understand. They are musical notes on the scale of human experience. Our task is, like an expert conductor, to use words and symbols in a way that first embraces the current thinking context of our audience and then calls for them to release it so that a higher order of thinking (and inspiration) can naturally emerge.

Inspiration in Action #15: Even mystics have hormones

Graves was a hard-boiled scientist. As such, he was mistrustful of metaphysical thinking. But for anyone with a background in world mythology, it's hard to overlook the striking parallels between Graves' developmental stages and the meanings ascribed to the Hindu 'chakras', or bodily energy systems. Starting with the first (or 'root') chakra [Graves level 2], up through the seventh (or 'crown') chakra [Graves level 8], the corresponding themes and life lessons line up perfectly. Was Graves using behavioral psychology to uncover truths that mystics had intuited thousands of years prior? Spooky, man.

CHAPTER 08

·····

EIGHT WAYS OF BEING HUMAN

·····

"If one does not understand a person, one tends to regard him as a fool." - Carl Jung

In this chapter we will take a closer look at each thinking system, highlighting the key mental context (values, attitudes, resonant metaphors and core assumptions about the nature of the world) for each. Once this framework sinks in, you'll understand how to naturally craft messages that resonate with your audience—any audience—from the inside out.

Before describing each level in greater detail, there are a few interpretative preliminaries to consider. First, each successive level represents a quantum leap forward in what is termed "cognitive complexity." Complexity is a scientific concept borrowed from systems theory referring to the level of *differentiation* and simultaneous *integration* of one's mental faculties, and is not a measure of intelligence. It turns out that IQ is (for the most part) statistically independent of cognitive complexity.

Also, while it is important to distinguish qualitative differences among these thinking levels, it is equally important to avoid judging any particular system as better or worse than another. Instead, each level can be seen as having healthy and unhealthy expressions. In its healthy state, each of the levels of existence spelled out on the next page plays an important role in the health of our society. To truly be of service, we must find and leverage everyone's unique strength, not judge their relative worth.

Finally, please note that these levels of existence are *ways* of thinking rather than *types* of people. Over the course of a given day, a person might experience any number of these thinking systems depending upon situational factors. While it is correct to say that most people have a habitually preferred level of operation, it would be a mistake to limit anyone to only one rung of the existential ladder. To define a person by their habitual thinking style is to confuse them with their mind. And this is the exact opposite of what we must do if we wish to inspire them.

....

Existential Level 1: *Autistic Thinking*

Color Code: Tan*

Date: Approx. 40,000 BCE and earlier

Life Theme: "Express self as an animal according to the dictates of urgent physiological needs." 7 [Theme statements quoted directly from Graves. See end notes.]

Life Goal: To find sustenance and satisfy biological imperatives.

Found Today: severely mentally challenged, cases of post traumatic shock (PTSD), brain injuries

....

Existential Level 2: *Tribal/Magical Thinking*

Color Code: Violet

Date: Approx. 40,000 BCE

Life Theme: "Sacrifice one's desires to the way of one's elders and ancestors."

Core Values: Safety, Tradition

Guiding Metaphor: Life is a sacrifice (and similar)

Life Goal: To please the spirits and ensure continuance of the tribe.

Illustrative Words: magic, spirits, incantations, ritual, sacrificial rites, favor of gods, superstition

---

* Graves' original naming system was somewhat cumbersome. In their book *Spiral Dynamics,* authors Don Beck and Christopher Cowan propose a simple color-coding scheme for identifying each existential level. Their approach has proven an ingenious shorthand for communicating about Graves' thinking levels. Because the present theoretical approach (Transformational Design®) is fundamentally distinct from Beck and Cowan's, I have chosen to adopt a distinct color scheme. For those who wish to attempt a cross-platform integration of various Gravesian research resources, I highly recommend you visit the 'Further Research' section on page 211.

Found Today: Australian Aborigines, ancient rites, Native American rituals, worldwide origin myths, shamanistic cults, world tribal cultures

....

EXISTENTIAL LEVEL 3: *Heroic Thinking*

Color Code: Crimson

Date: Approx. 8000 BCE

Life Theme: "Express one's self, to hell with consequences, lest one suffer the torment of shame."

Core Values: Power, Strength

Guiding Metaphor: Life is a battle (and similar)

Life Goal: To escape the suffocating dictates of tradition and achieve personal power/glory.

Illustrative Words: ruthless, raw, authoritarian, predatory, heroic, impulsive, misogynistic, legendary, violent, egocentric

Found Today: passionate dance forms, gangster rap, prison culture, sociopaths, dictators, drug cultures, religious extremists, extreme sports

....

EXISTENTIAL LEVEL 4: *Absolutistic Thinking*

Color Code: Navy

Date: Approx. 4000–2000 BCE

Life Theme: "Sacrifice self now to receive later reward."

Core Values: Discipline, Authority, Purpose

Guiding Metaphor: Life is a test (and similar)

Life Goal: To find peace and meaning in this world by denying impulses and upholding morality.

Illustrative Words: purity, one right way, immutable laws, God's will, deference, righteousness, chosen people, "tough cop" God-image

Found Today: The "moral majority," deep south of United States (aka "The Bible Belt"), the Vatican, Sarah Palin, the military, monks, accountants, "values voters," pro-life activists, fundamentalists (of every stripe)

EXISTENTIAL LEVEL 5: *Individualistic Thinking*

Color Code: Copper

Date: Approx. 1300–1400 CE

Life Theme: "Express self for what self-desires, but in a calculated fashion so as to avoid bringing down the wrath of important others."

Core Values: Accomplishing, Power, Profit

Guiding Metaphor: Life is a game, or world is a machine (and similar)

Life Goal: To achieve success and affluence in this life by strategically manipulating desired outcomes.

Illustrative Words: invisible hands, survival of the fittest, individualism, capitalism, competition, scientific method, objectivity, ends over means, social Darwinism, tough, scheming, skepticism, "God is dead"

Found Today: NAFTA, objectivists, Wall Street, China's economic boom, free-market economic theories, sales professionals, neocon imperialists, politicians of every stripe, book "The Fountainhead"

EXISTENTIAL LEVEL 6: *Humanistic Thinking*

Color Code: Jade

Date: Approx. 1900 CE

Life Theme: "Sacrifice self now in order to gain acceptance now."

Core Values: Equality, Honesty, Relatedness

Guiding Metaphor: Mankind is a family (and similar)

Life Goal: To find happiness in this life—in this moment—by relating deeply to other humans.

Illustrative Words: harmony, community, the human family, freedom of speech, warmth, softness, gentleness, charity, egalitarian views, civil rights, welfare concept, embracing subjectivity, idealism, kindness

Found Today: social media, National Public Radio (NPR), civil rights legislation, sensitivity training, socialism, "flaming liberals," ACLU, Burning Man gatherings, progressive cities like Seattle/San Francisco/Portland

....

EXISTENTIAL LEVEL 7: *Systemic Thinking*

Color Code: Gold

Date: Approx. 1950 CE (now emerging en masse)

Life Theme: "Express self for what self desires and others need, but never at the expense of others, and in a way that all life can continue to exist."

Core Values: Integrity, Competence, Sustainability

Guiding Metaphor: Life is a system (and similar)

Life Goal: To restore vitality and balance to a world torn asunder.

Illustrative Words: clarity, inspiration, vitality, insight, interdependence, emerging from embeddedness, resolving paradoxes, planetary vision, transformation, flexibility, "thrive and help thrive" ethic

Found Today: Apple, google, sustainability movement, LOHAS movement, deep ecology, Barack Obama, progressive politics, rise of the "cultural creatives", quantum theory, integral theory, innovative technologies

....

EXISTENTIAL LEVEL 8: *Holistic Thinking*

Color Code: Indigo

Date: In process

Life Theme: "Sacrifice the idea that one will ever truly know and adjust to this as the existential fact of existence."

Core Values: Experience, Humility, Reverence

Guiding Metaphor: Life is a dream (and similar)

Life Goal: To surrender to the spiritual dimension underlying all forms.

Illustrative Words: poetic perception, impressionism, transcendence, world as illusion, surrender, unseen order, temporary nature of forms, unity, integration, faith

Found Today: mystical tradition, fine art/poetry/music, spiritual book *A Course in Miracles*, the perennial philosophy, Buddhist concept 'maya'

....

This book is for Level 7

Which of these levels resonated most with your thinking? If I've done my homework correctly, you related most strongly to existential level number seven (systemic/gold thinking) and, to a lesser extent, levels six (humanistic/jade thinking) and eight (holistic/indigo thinking). How do I know this? Because I've used the very principles outlined in this book to design this book so that it will appeal to these specific mindsets!

In the interest of full transparency, I can now disclose that this book is actually a Level 7 communication manual, written to help the level 6's ('jades') and level 7's ('golds') of the world learn how to finally start communicating effectively with all other colors of the mental rainbow in the service of our one shared life. Inspiration, the effortless by-product of transformational communication, is only relevant because it is the experiential medium through which we will help humans at every level of

> **Inspiration in Action #16: Gold is the new green**
>
> Over the past few years, the so-called *green* movement has taken over. We've now got green houses, green clothes, green restaurants, green awards ceremonies...you name it. But are we to believe that this green romance is anything beyond a passing trend? The answer: absolutely, yes! The words may change, but the trend is just beginning. You see, unlike the more conservation-oriented environmentalists of yesterday, today's green leaders are solutions-focused systems thinkers and innovators…in other words, they are very 'gold.' The main reason that the new green movement will flourish is that a critical number of people are now thinking along the lines of this inspired systemic world view.
>
> The hippies were fun, but not nearly as focused, disciplined, and well-groomed.

complexity unlock their hidden psycho-spiritual potential in the service of the evolution of our species and life on this planet.

I feel so much better now that we've stopped pretending, don't you?

In all seriousness, I do respect and admire people who have the courage to engage this topic. To me, it says something inspiring about who you are in the world. It means you have a true commitment to life and a strong vision for the future. You sense that we need a new way of thinking and engaging the world if we want to fix the complex planetary problems that plague us. You are the progressives, visionaries, entrepreneurs, activists and artists that care enough to release self-righteousness and offer your talents in the service of something larger. I'm proud to know you.

The four American ways

If the good news is that you are part of mankind's emerging cognitively complex elite, the bad news is that the vast majority of our fellow Americans are still operating from less complex levels. Are they bad people? Are we superior? No! And please stop thinking that way! This whole exhausting conversation about superiority is one of our biggest obstacles to making progress—it assumes that our intention is to manipulate or take advantage. It assumes that scarcity is real and that trust isn't valid. If you want to have that kind of conversation, please do so elsewhere.

Here's the bottom line, as I see it: we need to improve the quality of the conversation if we want to make an impact. We need to let ourselves trust that although we are all equal in a spiritual sense, we are very different in terms of our cognitive styles and strategies. This isn't a value judgment, it's a fact of nature. Furthermore, these differences matter when it comes to communication. Why? Because differences in cognitive complexity determine the shape and size of the mental and spiritual filters that gauge our access to inner life energies.

Overall, how does today's mainstream American audience stack up on this scale? Although no hard data exists, we can extrapolate from Grave's research to paint a rough picture. The United States was originally settled by people of a predominantly level five (individualist/copper) and level four (absolutistic/navy) disposition. At the time, this represented the near cutting-edge of human consciousness. The result? America was able to craft a resilient democracy that has been a model of prosperity for the whole planet. The combination of absolutistic discipline and enterprising ambition has proven a sturdy, creative social concoction that has made the United States the most powerful kid on the block.

But times are changing, and we haven't been keeping step. Unchecked commercialism has damaged our integrity and stunted our forward growth. To correct these blockages and restore the balance, a systemic, inspirational revolution is currently underway. The problems caused by rampant individualist/copper thinking have inspired pockets of people (largely through social media networks and in progressive centers like New York, San Francisco and Portland) to embrace more sophisticated modes of thought.

Please see Figure 7 on the top of page 93. If we assumed a normal distribution of thinking types across the country, the distribution would probably look something like this curve.[8] The 'median' thinking type would be at the later stages of individualist/copper, slowly moving into the realm of humanistic/jade. A significant portion of our population still thinks in terms of absolutistic/navy, although most of these are now kicking and screaming as they learn the lessons of individualistic/

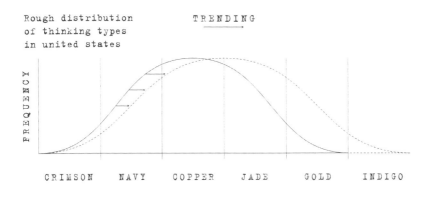

DISTRIBUTION OF GRAVES THINKING TYPES
FIGURE: 7

copper self-expression. At the tail ends of the distribution, we have a smaller percentage of heroic/crimson thinking types (as seen mostly in prison cultures and gangs) and systemic/gold thinking types (as seen in the environmental movement and the 'for benefit' business revolution).

But the complexity map of America is trending upward fast, bringing with it a whole host of inspired young people and aging discontents. The reason for this upshift is simple: survival. Given the environmental and economic challenges we face, evolving to 'gold' thinking has become a matter of survival necessity. What does this mean for our country? It means that we can expect the booming environmental, LOHAS, and progressive movements to spiral forward indefinitely. One way or another, systemic thinking must prevail if life is to continue.

What does this trend mean for us as inspirational communicators? It means that there will be a growing demand for people who can bridge the gap between these thinking systems and create solutions that work for everyone. Fear-based sales tactics and 'us versus them' political rhetoric are becoming outmoded as our country sheds the shackles of strict absolutistic/navy morality and individualist/copper profit myopia. In the decades ahead, inspiration will become an even more valuable commodity and authenticity will become the new norm.

Inspiration in Action #17: Giving is the new taking

Large corporations are now realizing that they must do whatever they can to infuse their brands with an air of generosity and authenticity. The result: cause-related marketing is all the rage! Why has being charitable suddenly become so chic? Because a collapsing dollar, a shrinking middle class and undrinkable tap water has caused many to question the wisdom of unchecked free-market capitalism. In other words, unrestrained 'copper' is on the way out. Expect to see humanism and service as growing themes in the media from now on, as copper thinkers slowly learn to think in a more systemic and humanistic way (or at least do their best to fake it for enhanced profits).

The big picture: putting Graves in context

Lest we forget, our sponsoring goal for this conversation is to learn how to inspire others. To do this we must be able to craft authentic messages that are perceived as personally relevant—this requires that we be willing and able to see the world through our audience's eyes and grasp the deeper values and assumptions that underlie their specific worldviews.

Understanding these core ways of thinking is the first step. Remember, the mind is always a means, never an end. Regardless of thinking type, we must always try to take our audience through the same underlying process. But, to accomplish this feat in the real world, we must deeply grasp the inner landscape of at least the four dominant value systems that populate the American consciousness at this moment in history.

In the following chapters we will spend some quality time with the absolutistic/navy, individualist/copper, humanistic/jade, and systemic/gold thinking types. Once you get these four contexts firmly established in your mind, you will never again be able to watch TV or read the newspaper without seeing them at play. Nor, as a communicator, will it be easy to ever again impose your own values and assumptions upon people who see the world through a much different set of lenses.

CHAPTER 09

.....

Inspiring the Absolutistic (Navy) Thinker

.....

"Moral courage is the most valuable and usually the most absent characteristic in men." - George Patton (navy General)

Vital Stats

Existential Level 4: Absolutistic Thinking (Code: Navy)

Date of Origin: Approx. 4000–2000 BCE

Gravesian Theme: "Sacrifice self now to receive later reward."

Core Values: Discipline, Authority, Purpose

Guiding Metaphor: Life is a test (and similar)

Goal: To find peace and meaning in this world by denying impulses and upholding moral laws.

Representative Examples: George W. Bush, Sarah Palin, James Dobson, "Values Voters," Moral Majority, John Wayne archetype, fundamentalists of any stripe (Christian, Muslim, Jewish, atheistic, financial, academic)

Basic Navy Credo

"Life is a test in which I must prove myself worthy by sacrificing my own desires and delaying immediate gratification. To accomplish this I must uphold absolute, properly sanctioned laws."

General Observations

The absolutistic thinking system is a tough nut to crack. Of all levels of thinking, it is the most paradoxical. As Graves was fond of noting, people who think this way are at once gentle and warlike, self-righteous and insecure. To empathize with this way of thinking we must understand that this approach to life was crafted from a deep sense of existential insecurity. Navy thinkers cannot tolerate uncertainty—they have an unassailable need for clear, unambiguous answers to life's deepest questions.

Once we grasp this, we can begin to look past their iron-tough facade and appreciate the soft, disarming nature of navy's inner spirit. Also, we can begin to notice areas in our life where we personally choose to adopt absolutistic thinking in order to deal with threatening issues (religious, political, family, romantic, etc.). This can help us become more appreciative and compassionate towards those who think this way.

Why did absolutist navy thinking originate?

The birth of this thinking system coincides with the birth of all major monotheistic religions worldwide. Today many cynics view religion with a jaundiced eye because of the hypocritical holy wars that have been perpetrated on behalf of religion. But cynics often fail to realize what a major advancement this approach to living represents for our species as a whole. The absolute right and wrong worldview was a quantum leap of mankind's consciousness to help resolve the problems of violence and chaos that plagued early man.

The early warrior human (level three) was unable to control his impulses and too often allowed his need for power and pleasure to override his humanity. This left him with a gaping sense of meaninglessness and an inability to feel connected to his inner spirit. Religion filled this void and provided a ground-breaking matrix through which humans could come together in the service of a common good. For many people in our country and around the world, it still serves this function admirably.

The mass emergence of navy thinking represented the first time in human history that existential questions were successfully articulated into massive coordinated political organizations with transcendent values like 'freedom' and 'justice.' Even today, healthy navy thinking is the backbone of a healthy functioning society. Mass monetary and legal systems would be meaningless without at least a passing acceptance of absolutistic navy morality and impulse control.

Core characteristics of navy

Navy thinking is held together by a few powerful threads. First, these thinkers have an ambivalent relationship to authority. At a core level they desire the clarity of an absolute authority to tell them what it right and wrong. At a shadow level they resent the suffocating restrictions that such authority puts on their individual self-expression. As a result, we often find them to be closed and hostile towards virtually every kind of authority except their one chosen, absolutely correct one. Sound familiar?

For example, evangelical Christian (navy) fundamentalists will often believe almost anything the Bible (or their preacher) says with unswerving faith. However, confront the individual with compelling evidence from scientific authorities, and you will likely get a smug, uninterested, or even angry response. The reverse also holds true. Dogmatic scientists are often unmoved by anything religious, no matter how potentially enlightening or uplifting. Both are operating from the same tough, extreme, absolutistic thinking style. Navy thinking always chooses an absolute authority and defends itself against any outside influence. This can make the navy mind very difficult to persuade or inspire, unless you can successfully represent yourself as a messenger for their preferred vendor of absolute truth.

Navy thinkers demonstrate a tremendous in-group bias. They will give everything—even their own lives—for people with the same beliefs as them. At the same time, they may show complete apathy or hostility to those who they identify as 'other.' The most confusing thing here is that sometimes the other is identical in almost every observable way! A minor disagreement about some piddling religious doctrine or governmental policy becomes a valid reason to attack and/or dehumanize another party. Even more confusing is that these are often the same people who preach loudly about charity and service to mankind!

Navy can seem infuriating when we witness the blaring contradiction between its actions and stated beliefs. But when we look without judgement at its dark existential conundrum, we see that everything navy does and says lines up with its one core unsatisfied need—to feel safe and secure in a 'dangerous' world. The unquestioned worship of one absolute authority, the irrational in-group bias, the blaring contradiction between beliefs and actions, all derive from a need to feel safe. We can argue with such people until we're blue (or navy) in the face, but it won't make a difference because they aren't interested in discovering truth. They are interested in proving that they already know it. To navy thinking, curiosity is a luxury; safety is the thing.

Lest we paint a one-sided picture, we should also consider the profound gifts that this thinking system brings. The birth of navy is the birth of discipline and the birth of moral society. All of the major advancements of the modern world were made possible by the hard-working navy sacrificial ethic. Without discipline and a basic sense of morality, a society cannot move past tyranny and the inner spirit of man cannot flourish. Psychology has shown that children raised without at least a moderate amount of navy mental training (discipline and the capacity to delay gratification) rarely achieve happy, fulfilling lives.

In the end, inspiring the navy saintly mind has more to do with appreciating and leveraging its gifts than with criticizing its weaknesses. This thinking system, like all systems, has both healthy and unhealthy manifestations. Inspired and healthy navy is a humble, tireless ally.

Healthy navy: The model American

When they feel safe and appreciated, navy thinkers are some of the most hard-working and dutiful members of our species. They will toil with missionary zeal in the pursuit of common objectives with little or no expectation for personal gain. They will spontaneously offer to help others in crisis. They will show steadfast strength and resolve for their beliefs, their families and their countries. This is because they trust, without question, that their lives are meant to serve something greater, and that man was born a noble righteous being with a larger purpose for living. Navy thinkers take life seriously and are eager to demonstrate their earnest passions in the world through causes that truly matter.

Unhealthy navy: The angry nut job

When they feel unsafe, navy thinkers can be terrifying. Furthermore, it doesn't take much to trip the deep existential angst-wire at their core, leading to all manner of controlling behavior and hateful warlike tendencies endemic of the earlier heroic/crimson thinking system (level three).

Racist cults like the KKK, the Nazi movement, abortion clinic bombers and gay-bashing Christian coalitions are but a few examples of horrifying movements that emerge when unhealthy navy tries to take charge. In their own minds, unhealthy navy thinkers are actually on a noble quest to purify and redeem mankind's lost soul. Make no mistake: these people are not stupid, they are scared and misguided. In the absence of a trusted authority, they take it upon themselves to create a purpose in which they and their fellow believers must forge salvation in a dirty, unsafe world. Lord help you if you fall into the wrong socio-demographic category.

Inspiration in action #18: Portrait of a navy leader

In his 1984 reelection campaign, Ronald Reagan ran what has become considered one of the most inspired political ads ever. Titled "Morning in America," this commercial radiates all the purity and optimism of a Normal Rockwell painting. Like Reagan himself, this media was a perfect representation of navy optimism and hope. Instead of tackling complex issues head-on, this commercial created a simple resonant vision, employing the metaphor of a sunrise that evoked the deep 'navy' sense of absolute faith in eternity. Historians and pundits may argue over the end-value of Reagan's policies, but one cannot deny the power of the inspired optimism he elicited, as embodied in this now legendary advertisement.

How does navy see America?

Navy thinking Americans generally feel that America is on the verge of collapse. Interestingly, true democracy is a threatening concept to navy thinking because it places authority in the hands of the masses rather than in the hands of a 'properly sanctioned' authority. The irony in America in the first decade of this century was that our most overtly 'patriotic' citizens are also the ones who most deeply fear the democratic process!

Historically speaking, navy thinking is generally patriotic in a "love it or leave it" sort of way. Until George W. Bush came into office in 2000, navy thinkers generally had a very negative view of the direction that America was heading. Because he is such a strong proponent of absolutistic navy thinking, Bush's election represented a huge achievement and a cause for celebration and hope. "Finally, someone who understands the truth and will restore moral order to our crumbling world!" Navy thinkers rejoiced.

Unfortunately, a government run by a navy-minded President did not flourish in a complex 21st century world, and the Bush legacy collapsed in miserable ineptitude. So has America's global reputation, the Republican party, our military and our once sprawling economy.

In the world at large, we see navy just now emerging in many third world countries. The spread of Christianity in war-torn parts of Africa is just one great example. To people living in a might-makes-right warrior culture, this is a wonderful development and a huge leap forward.

Inspiration in action #19: Portrait of a navy brand

Researchers estimate that ninety-nine percent of American consumers can identify the Prudential logo upon first sight. This wide-spread recognition is partly due to this company's marketing power and longevity, but—at a deeper level—drives from the primal cognitive associations that this ingenious brand evokes. A large, unmoving rock is a particularly inspired metaphor for a company that seeks to give its customers a sense of absolute security and trust. This brand perfectly symbolizes the absolutistic navy thinker in all of us, seeking for clean, pure, unambiguous answers to life's problems.. When it comes to financial security and safety, who wouldn't like to own a piece of the rock?

Here in the United States, things are different. The navy system is pretty much the low man on the existential totem-pole. This has given many American navy thinkers a massive inferiority complex such that even the use of college-level words by our leaders is considered valid evidence of cultural elitism!

How does navy see other thinking systems?

Navy tends to view other major American thinking systems (and strangers, in general) with a mixture of moral judgment and repressed envy.

Navy Meets Individualism/Copper (Level 5):
Navy thinkers usually have both judgment and admiration for copper's individualism. At one level they resent copper's 'moral depravity,' at another level they secretly long for the same. Once a navy thinker decides to stop fearing authority and repressing his 'sinful' urges, he will stop judging copper thinkers and forgive himself for being imperfect. This will pave the way for his progress to the next existential level. Copper thinkers can be great mentors for navy thinkers at this volatile transitional stage.

Navy Meets Humanism/Jade (Level 6):
Navy usually despises the fuzziness of jade humanism. Navy needs clarity, not 'psychobabble,' 'liberalism,' and 'moral relativism.' Navy sees jade's relativistic worldview as wishy-washy. For navy, the worst thing about jade humanism is that it places human authority and immediate gratification above absolute authority and long-term salvation. To navy, the lack of requisite character and discipline required to stifle hedonistic impulses and embrace 'family values' is the major cause of our country's crumbling moral infrastructure.

Navy Meets Systemic Thinking/Gold (Level 7):
Navy doesn't trust gold, but for reasons it cannot explain. Existentially speaking, gold thinkers are vastly more complex. They have reached a stage where they are relatively fearless and are no longer in need of ideology to feel secure. Gone is the wishy-washy quality of jade

humanism, but still strongly intact is the desire to serve. Gone is the manipulative quality of copper individualism, but still intact is the ability to get things done. Navy thinkers do not understand this, and usually keep their uneasiness at bay by judging gold as arrogant.

Who does navy trust?

Navy thinkers trust anyone who can confirm their sacrificial values and give them a sense of direction—usually an authority that is historically sanctioned. Always remember, navy thinkers are desperately in need of a transcendent purpose to justify the suffering of this world. This could be the promise of a happy afterlife ('heaven'), or a happy later-life (religious cultural dominance), but the purpose must seem clear, solid and urgent. Anyone who can provide them with this will attain their tireless loyalty. Did you ever wonder why Karl Rove was so successful at getting Republicans elected? He knew how to give navy-thinkers a sense of purpose by inventing threatening wedge issues (gay marriage, prayer in schools, etc.) to activate their inner need for security and righteousness. Fortunately his lack of authenticity has ultimately undermined Republican credibility and leverage with the navy 'values-based' voting constituency.

Tips for designing inspiring navy communications

Although every situation is unique, here are some principles that I've found useful when designing media and communications intended to inspire people who identify with an absolutistic thinking style.

STEP #1: ENGAGE THE NAVY SENSORY FILTER:

As always, make sure to design your message with an aesthetic quality, tone, and style that resonates with the navy sensibilities of your audience. Be creative. Choose a medium and distribution method that will stand out from the crowd and capture their senses. In general, navy thinkers are sensitive to visual designs that feel solid, reliable, and steeped in tradition. The navy thinker takes comfort in designs that reflect a sense of strength and solidity. Avoid being too flashy, avant- garde, or otherwise unfamiliar.

Inspiration in Action #20: Portrait of a navy movie

In 2004, Mel Gibson's "The Passion of the Christ"—an NC-17 rated, subtitled, blood-soaked depiction of a good man being brutalized—broke many all-time box office records. While most Hollywood types chalked this success up to the power of Christian 'franchising', a closer look reveals deeper psychological forces at work...namely, the mythic allure of martyrdom. "The Passion of the Christ" is the consummate navy martyr myth. To navy thinking, martyrs are the ultimate heroes because they are suffering for us, to redeem us for our inherent flaws (such as the notion of 'original sin'). The problem is that if one doesn't agree with the original assumption that we are all inherently flawed and must be saved, then the bloody suffering can seem simply tragic and its worship can seem more than a little warped and masochistic. It's all a matter of perspective.

Step #2: Engage the Navy Mental Filter:

The navy mind is always scanning the environment for two things: moral issues and the presence of legitimate authority. Whatever your message, first be aware that navy thinkers will not take you seriously unless they first establish that you are a sanctioned authority. Make this very clear early on, with references, degrees, and whatever else your audience holds as sacred.

Navy thinkers are very sensitive to moral challenges and desperately need to feel on the 'right' (or righteous) side of every issue. They view the world as a clear struggle between opposites: good vs. bad, us vs. them, science vs. religion, right vs. wrong. In fact, the navy mind is so sensitive to moral infringement that it usually won't feel comfortable unless it has a clear enemy to channel its passions against. Take this enemy fetish into council as you fashion your strategic approach.

Employ the techniques of situational and value framing covered in Chapter 3. One great tactic is to use the situation in which the media will be experienced (church, sports bar, cable show, etc.) as a springboard, using words and images that create the sense of a battle for or against their core values of discipline, authority and purpose.

At first this may seem manipulative, but it needn't be. The important thing is that we use this framing for authentic intentions. Remember, if we don't generate interest, we are not going to inspire anyone. If we create the sense of a war against cherished values, we will get the navy mind excited with a sense of purpose. Yes, this is the very same strategy with which the deviously clever strategist Karl Rove managed to get George Bush elected two times, but it could also be the approach we use to inspire Christians to embrace a progressive environmental agenda. It can work both ways.

Another powerful tactic is to apply resonant metaphors. Navy thinkers view the world as a test that they must pass. Use this metaphor to get the navy mind engaged. Whatever your initiative, make it a challenge in which the navy-thinking audience must prove themselves worthy. This will give them a sense of purpose and motivate them to harness their considerable passion towards your cause.

Besides these tactics, feel free to draw from any number of the other mind-capturing strategies covered in Chapter 3 (*questioning, problem making, personal recognition, storytelling, etc.*). The important thing is that you cater these communication tactics to the particular values and goals of an absolutistic/navy thinking audience.

Step #3: Overcoming the Navy Spiritual Filter:
Once we've got the navy mind engaged, we can take it to the next level. In accordance with the principle of context, our design goal is now to help the person recontextualize their experience into something more inspiring and profound. We can do this by any combination of the following approaches: *listening* (if applicable), *telling unspoken truths, considering limiting metaphors, introducing transformational metaphors, humor, rhythm and rhyme, story payoffs, solutions, calls to duty, calls to action, calls to imagine,* and/or *silence*. My personal favorite tactics involve using questions to address metaphors.

The dominant navy metaphor for life is a test. This metaphor has certain limitations: it forces the person to constantly wonder if they are getting a passing or failing grade. Navy thinkers constantly feel judged by some hidden authority that they cannot directly see. The buried guilt is tremendous! If you want to give a navy audience a true taste of freedom, use words and questions in a way that calls into question the validity of this hidden organizing framework or context. "What would you do if failure was impossible?" "Are you tired of always trying to live up to an impossible standard?" "What if there's nothing wrong with being wrong?" The possibilities are infinite. The goal is to invite the person to consider life outside the existing metaphor.

A follow-up process that can be even more powerful is to introduce the transformational metaphor—the metaphor employed by the next higher existential level. For navy, the next stage of complexity is individualism/copper, which operates according to the game metaphor. Use words, images, and symbols to cause your navy audience to adopt a view of life as a game. This can ignite in them a tremendous sense of liberation, as if a huge burden has been lifted. Games have winners and losers, but games are temporary (not absolute) and less threatening than tests. Most of all, games are fun.

Another particularly potent way to inspire navy thinkers is with a call to duty. The navy worldview is based upon duty and the belief that we are all called to sacrifice ourselves to a larger purpose. If you can get the navy mind to consider that we are presenting it with a genuine call to duty, inspiration and motivation will surely follow.

At a worldly level, we could call them to sacrifice their gas guzzling trucks; at a spiritual level we could call them to sacrifice their need to sacrifice their own will to higher authority. (How's that for a paradox!?) However we frame it, sacrifice inspires navy. If we are authentic and if we frame our message to their sacrificial listening, an open spiritual filter will inevitably result.

When absolutists transform into individualists...

When fresh insights add enough space and energy to the navy thinking system, the individual releases this sacrificial worldview and sheds the shackles of dogmatic conformity. The person is born into a new world where they are free to create and express whatever excites them. It's a magnificent transformation to behold. Unfortunately, this newfound confidence comes with a new set of existential challenges. Copper thinkers are no longer moved by sacrifice to authority and morality. Buckle up, because inspiring clever individualists can be a much tougher challenge.

CHAPTER 10

·····

Inspiring the Individualistic (Copper) Thinker

·····

"A man fully in possession of his mind may rightly acquire anything else to which he is justly entitled."
- Andrew Carnegie (copper tycoon)

Vital Stats

Existential Level 5: Individualistic Thinking (Code: Copper)

Date of Origin: Approx. 1300–1400 CE

Gravesian Theme: "Express self for what self-desires, but in a calculated fashion so as to avoid bringing down the wrath of important others."

Core Values: Accomplishing, Power, Profit

Guiding Metaphor: Life is a game or world is a machine (and similar)

Goal: To achieve success and affluence in this life by strategically accomplishing desired outcomes.

Representative Examples: Karl Rove, Donald Trump, Anthony Robbins, Margaret Thatcher, Wall Street executives, Dick Cheney, Gordon Gecko, Paris Hilton, Enron, Willie Loman, Rudy Giuliani, Ayn Rand

Basic Copper Credo

"Life is a competitive game in which I must achieve my goals in whatever way I can without getting into trouble. To win, I must truly understand the value of personal power."

General observations

The individualistic 'copper' mindset is a hearty, creative, clever and resourceful approach to living. Almost all political and technological advancement since the Renaissance has been made possible by this bold leap in human thinking. At this existential stage, the individual is still quite strongly identified with the material world as real and important. As a result, material affluence, physical beauty and/or worldly power are often highly cherished ends. Unlike navy, copper doesn't want some respected authority to tell it how to live—it wants to be that respected authority!

The key to understanding people who think this way is to realize that you can't always trust what they are telling you to be what they truly believe. Integrity for copper is not so much about saying the factual truth, as it's about staying true to their own agenda. The guilt that such a morally slippery mindset creates inside the individual is often projected outward in the form of competitiveness, compulsiveness and disregard for the whole 'icky' inner realm of feelings. This keeps the individual locked up emotionally and presents us with a unique communication challenge: we must invite the copper-minded individual to recontextualize self-interest in a more expansive way. First and foremost, this requires that we demonstrate genuine compassion and respect for the copper mindset, with its unique strengths and contributions. It also requires that we be unafraid to be tough, when necessary, to push through the beastly copper ego.

Why did copper originate?

Greek philosopher Heraclitus boldly proclaimed that, "War is the father of all things." If so, then we might view copper thinking as the existential offspring of the war between mankind's inner need for security and his need to be free from all rules. When the mammoth morality-based religions began to dominate the cultural and political life of man, his life conditions improved tremendously. Protected from predators and starvation, he began to question the prudence of waiting until heaven to experience bliss. Eventually his patience for dogma wore thin, and he decided to take matters into his own existential hands.

Science was born. Art and literature flourished. Higher education proliferated. Production became automated, and commerce became global. Copper thinking provided a seductive solution to the problems of repressed, saintly man—embrace personal wealth and enjoyment in the here and now as symbolic expressions of God's love for the morally righteous few (see Benjamin Franklin's writings for a great example of this sort of navy-emerging-copper thinking). Over the centuries, the 'God' part of the equation has dwindled for most. Today, we find copper as a creative force of industry, seeking profit and power for their own sake, without the need for godly rationalizations.

Core characteristics of copper

Copper thinking is pragmatic and self-directed. More complex than the warrior-like 'might-makes-right' ethic of early man, copper thinking understands morality and considers others before taking action. But if we look more closely, we'll usually see that such 'consideration' has little to do with concern for the welfare of others, and much to do with the percieved impact of other's actions upon personal goals. As a rule, the copper mind views people through the strategic filter of personal ambitions.

Many self-righteous liberal types off-handedly dismiss copper thinking as the scourge of the earth, as the cause of mankind's spreading social and environmental ills. But the truth is copper thinking isn't inherently bad or good—it is just a way of thinking and operating in the world. If we are disenchanted by copper's unhealthy impact on our planet (through pollution, sweat shops and wealth hoarding), we must find a way to channel its actions in a positive direction. The first step is to forgive our grievances and understand that everything copper does results from noble—if sometimes short-sighted—intentions.

Here's the scoop: Copper thinkers believe that humans are strong, self-determined beings. To indulge in debased concepts such as victimhood and to give handouts to the needy offends copper's deepest sensibilities about the inherently creative, powerful nature of our species. Copper thinking accepts that tough lessons are sometimes a healthy part of the natural growth process. People learn toughness by falling on their face and getting back up again. For copper, to love people is to respect and encourage their strength, not to pander to them like they're a helpless bunch of weaklings. Copper believes that each of us is responsible for creating our own lives.

To copper, life is a game—a rough, exciting game that we are all here to play full out. To win this game, one must fashion a successful and abundant life in the here and now. It is an invigorating worldview for those able to embrace it. It's also morally seductive, because the copper thinker is no longer forced to emotionally digest the suffering present among his fellow humans. Guilt can be simply written off as weakness, and poverty blamed on the poor. The primal human impulse to serve others can be rationalized away through abstract theories about "trickle-down economics" and "invisible hands." The individual uses the mind for a dual purpose: to create material affluence and to stave off a deep sense of loneliness. This dual mind is the source of copper's duplicitous tendencies and also the eventual cause of its emotional undoing.

Unfortunately, even the richest and most famous of tycoons must come to grips with their own mortality. When the reality of mortality hits, a copper-thinker may begin to once again wonder about that part of his nature that is beyond form. In America, this is typified by the spiritual breakthrough that follows a successful mid-life crisis, but can theoretically occur at any stage of the human life cycle.

Healthy copper: the generous entrepreneur

When they are in control and flourishing, copper thinkers are some of the most prolific and generous leaders of our society. Healthy copper thinkers infect others with their boundless optimism and vision. They create companies, jobs and technology—the very economic infrastructure that sustains capitalism. They have an uncanny ability to sense opportunity and can lead others to greatness. They are motivators with boundless energy and unmatched persuasive abilities. They truly understand the power of the human will, and can effectively call others to embrace and express their own personal power as well. The morality learned from navy helps healthy copper express its own need for profit in a balanced way, to the benefit of all of us.

Unhealthy copper: the selfish bastard

In times of crisis, when copper thinkers lose control, it's a dark sight to behold. Without a sense of control, copper finds itself in an untenable position: exposed and vulnerable in a competitive, dangerous world.

The copper thinker is left with a choice: should he ask for help from other humans and risk being vulnerable, or simply push harder to achieve his goals? For unhealthy copper, the answer is clear: Push! Push! Push! Achieving success and social prestige becomes an almost messianic quest for inner-fulfillment, a surrogate for human warmth.

Over time, the unhealthy copper smile becomes a scowl. Nothing is enough. People become pawns and life loses its luster. The more the unhealthy copper mind admits to the loss of its own happiness, the more it tries to compensate with symbols of material power. At later stages, we commonly find people of this mindset using alcohol and drugs to stave off loneliness and a foreboding sense of doom.[9]

How does copper see America?

Copper thinkers and America go together like peas and carrots. The United States was founded by relatively healthy and hearty individualists

---

Inspiration in Action #21: Portrait of a copper self-promoter

Call him an ass or a genius, but one thing you can definitely say about Donald Trump is this: he is the very archetype of an individualistic/copper thinker. From his self-named towers in midtown Manhattan, to his 2007 book "Think Big and Kick Ass in Business and Life" (no kidding), Donald Trump embodies the acquisitive and self-promoting brand of American industriousness to which many today still aspire. Ever on a mission to own things, in March of 2004 Trump applied for a trademark on the phrase "You're Fired!", to capitalize on the success of his then hit television show *The Apprentice*. Unfortunately the application didn't go through, and soon thereafter, low ratings caused him to withdraw from the show all-together so as to avoid hearing these same words from NBC execs.

seeking to escape old-world religious and political imperatives to create a new life of religious freedom and (tax-free) prosperity. The very US Constitution embodies copper thinking at its idealistic best.

Today, copper thinkers tend to enjoy America for a much more practical reason—because they own it! And, besides, it's still a pretty good place to do business. This is a country where almost anyone with the drive and stomach for the game can achieve great material success. All one needs is a good idea, a strategic mind and relentless ambition. Once a person succeeds, the government does its best to keep corporate costs down, by ensuring a massive supply of cheap immigrant labor and—if necessary—an easy path to outsourcing jobs overseas. The luckiest and most well-connected of copper thinkers even get money directly out of the taxpayers' pockets in the form of subsidies and thick no-bid government contracts.

At the end of the day, copper loves America and has done a pretty decent job of keeping its values and policy makers in line with its core agenda: to create unlimited wealth within a market free of the financial burdens of excess taxation and social/environmental accountability.

How does copper see other thinking systems?

Copper generally views all other systems through a pragmatic lens. "How will the people who think this way help me or hurt me in my quest to accomplish my goals?"

Copper Meets Absolutism/Navy (Level 4):
Copper thinkers appreciate how loyal, sacrificial and easily led navy thinkers can be. Healthy navy thinkers make great spouses, customers, and employees (as long as they can be made to refrain from expressing excessive moral outrage at copper values). Secretly, unhealthy copper despises dogma and authority of all sorts and pities navy's gullible nature. On the other hand, healthy copper-thinkers can make the best possible navy mentors, because they truly understand the navy existential predicament and can help them tackle it without undo fear. This sort of partnership can be deeply fulfilling for both parties.

Copper Meets Humanism/Jade (Level 6):

Copper thinkers can find jade thinkers to be moderately or highly unpleasant. First of all, jade thinkers are frustratingly difficult for copper to control because they are operating from more complex, relativistic worldview. Also, jade thinkers often seem to copper more interested in having meetings and "sharing" than with getting things done. (*Note:* The term "bleeding heart" is a long favored phrase for tough-minded copper when describing softhearted, empathetic jade humanists.)

But, for copper, the most distasteful trait of jade thinking is that it constantly seems to be trying to make everyone feel guilty. Jade's humanistic values offend copper's belief in rugged individualism and stir the buried guilt around copper's spiritual filter. On the positive side, wealthy, successful jade thinkers make the perfect mentors for copper thinkers ready to seek out a more meaningful existence.

Copper Meets Systemic Thinking/Gold (Level 7):

Copper has an ambivalent, but generally positive relationship to gold thinking. Copper respects real-world results and sees that gold can generate massive profits and get things done without sacrificing its own conscience or being weak. At the same time, copper thinkers can be deeply jealous of gold thinkers because of their ability to relate openly and authentically with others. At the end of the day, gold is a great role model and mentor for any copper mind ready to integrate planetary and humanistic concerns into its ever-pressing self-oriented bottom line.

Who does copper trust?

Trust is the primary existential issue that copper thinkers must overcome in order to move forward. Because the copper mindset is opportunistic and calculating, it naturally assumes that the world is populated with mostly opportunistic and calculating people. No wonder it can't trust! In unhealthy copper, mistrust can lead to paranoia and delusions of persecution. But in most, mistrust lies just hidden in the background of awareness, as a faint sense that the world is not safe and a

> ### Inspiration in action #22: Portrait of a copper brand
>
> The remarkable thing about so-called copper systems (companies, governments, people, etc.) is how effectively they propagate themselves across time and space. In business, the idea of franchising is a consummately copper concept. No brand better illustrates this concept than McDonald's. When Ray Kroc opened this franchise in the 1950's, he tapped into the same pragmatic, industrious sort of copper thinking that led Henry Ford to invent the Model T. Optimistic, systematic and utterly sanitized, McDonald's represents the best and the worst of capitalistic America's 'copper' ideological underpinnings.

feeling that we must all watch our backs lest someone place a knife in it.

But, like everyone, copper has a soft and lovable underbelly. Trusted friends and associates know this side and are gifted with a less guarded version of copper's generous nature, especially in times of need. Copper-thinkers feel comforted by people who are "on their team." This comfort can develop into genuine admiration if these same individuals have also managed to achieve worldly success and prestige while also demonstrating higher attributes of emotional openness and warmth.

Tips for designing inspiring copper communications

Here are some general principles that I've found useful when designing media and communications to reach people who identify with the copper values and worldview.

Step #1: Engage the Copper Sensory Filter:
As always, make sure to design your message with an aesthetic quality, tone, and style that resonates with the copper sensibilities of your audience. Copper thinkers generally appreciate designs that project status, power, and strength. Copper thinkers want to stand out from the crowd, so their media should too. In choosing tone and feel, be light on tradition but conventional enough to evoke a sense of familiarity. In other words, be bold while staying somewhat within the bounds of convention. Avoid flowery or sappy aesthetics. Although copper thinking spans gender, it is an inherently masculine psychology.

STEP #2: ENGAGE THE COPPER MENTAL FILTER:

The copper mind is always scanning for opportunities to further its preset goals. Once you've got its attention, you must be quick and to the point. Copper thinkers must feel that what you have to say is factual, concrete, and vital to their self-interest (physical, financial, professional, social, etc.). The more you know about your audience's goals the better. In general, copper thinkers are enamored with new things and embrace quality tools for self improvement.

Situational framing can build resonance. If possible, cater your content to the specific situation in which the media will be distributed. What is the likely reason that your audience is in the type of location where the communication is taking place? What does this tell you about them? How are you going to help them? Framed effectively this sort of information will get the copper mind engaged.

Value framing is also critical. If possible, the message content should be framed according to copper values of accomplishing, power and profit. How are you creating an opportunity to help the copper mind accomplish things more easily? Take some time to imagine yourself in copper's shoes: What are some specific stresses and thoughts that might be happening in the mind of someone with that particular value system at that particular moment? The copper mind must feel that you understand and respect its values and that you have something of practical significance to offer it. Not breezy philosophy, but brass tacks, real-world stuff. Be concrete.

As always, resonant metaphors are powerful and can be used on both a visual and a verbal level. One great strategy is to create a challenge that the copper thinker must *win*. Sports metaphors can work wonders. In fact, competitive copper so loves a challenge that one great way to motivate it is by telling copper that it *can't* do something. Reverse psychology often goes a long, long way.

Understand that copper competitiveness is actually a by product of a fervent belief in the scarcity principle—the notion that this world is a zero-sum game. You might tactfully leverage copper's fear of being seen as a loser to get its attention, but be careful with this one. Fear is a real inspiration killer if you aren't using it delicately and with larger, life-serving intent.

Besides the strategies given, feel free to creatively draw from any number of the other proven mind capturing strategies covered in Chapter 3 (*questioning, problem making, personal recognition, storytelling*, etc). The important thing is that you artfully cater these communication tactics to the particular values and goals of your self-directed, individualistic copper audience.

Step #3: Overcome the Copper Spiritual Filter:

Once we've got the copper mind engaged, we can take it to the next level. Our design goal is now to help the person recontextualize their experience into something more expansive. We can do this by any combination of the approaches outlined in Chapter 3.

My personal favorite tactic for overcoming the copper spiritual filter is with strategic questions. This is true for all thinking types, but especially for copper, with its defensive, pragmatic, and mercurial mind. A good question will actually stop the mind for a moment and help the individual experience a moment of stillness from which inspiration can emerge. This question must be deeply rooted in an understanding of copper's unique psychological predicament.

On the surface, copper seems driven to achieve. On a hidden level, copper longs to feel accepted and loved. Knowing this structural contradiction, it is possible to create a question that inspires copper to consider, for example, that they truly *can* have material success and intimacy at the same time. A good question of this sort will open copper up to new possibilities. Once the door opens a crack, inspiration will keep leaking in and an indelible mental impression will be made. A great application of this principle comes from skillfully combining questions with metaphors, as described below.

The copper game metaphor is limiting. It causes one to constantly view other people through the lens of competition. To pave the

Inspiration in Action #23: Portrait of a copper movie

The story of copper's existential conundrum has been well-documented in myths, novels, and films throughout the past century. A breathtaking modern example comes from the Oscar winning film "There Will Be Blood" released in 2007. In this film, actor Daniel Day Louis plays an ambitious early 20th century oil tycoon who uses, befriends, and ultimately abandons a young boy left homeless and orphaned by an oil drilling accident. As this story progresses, the main character's trust issues and resistance towards the realm of introspection and feelings provides a poignant portrayal of the immense challenge copper thinkers undergo when life calls them to look inward at long repressed guilt.

way for the establishment of a new context that transcends the self/other polarity, urge your audience to consider these hidden limitations. "Aren't you tired of always having to stay one-up on the competition?" "Do ever feel that the cost of winning is just too great?" "What would you do if losing was impossible?" "What in your life is more valuable than winning?" Questions like this, applied in a context of deep rapport and trust, can be powerful indeed.

A complementary approach is to invite the copper audience to consider transformational metaphors. According to Graves research, the next higher evolutionary mental stage is humanistic/jade. Jade's favorite metaphor is the *human family.* If you can get copper to consider recontextualizing winners and losers as part of one family, you will be inviting them to see through the lens of a more complex worldview. This will give them a feeling of connectedness and expanded mental space (aka "inspiration"). But please be warned: this approach must not be tried unless you are being authentic. You can't manipulate someone into spiritual growth. Not only is it a creepy thing to do, it doesn't work. Manipulation has no leverage. Plus, copper is very sensitive to manipulation of all types and will see your effort as a strategic attempt to cause guilt, which (believe it or not) it actually is!

Another great tool for inspiring copper is with a call for action. The idea of action works well with copper, because it gets the copper imagination moving towards the immediacy of concrete, visualizable outcomes. If you can use this call to cause copper to foresee a credible vision that melds personal and collective success, you will surely inspire. The repressed unconscious copper guilt will abate, making room for a transformational experience to unfold.

When individualists transform into humanists...

When inspiration adds enough energy to the copper thinking system, the individual feels safe to release their agenda and open up to something new. The person experiences a fresh new world where they are no longer afraid to let their guard down, where their impact on other people matters, and where feelings are a vital part of being human. Interestingly enough, this surge of insight often comes with a newfound distaste for worldly ambition. As the individual embraces a jade value system, his disdain for the realm of inner-feelings may flip and become redirected towards the realm of unrestrained commercialism. Great communicators must understand this shift, and adjust their messages accordingly.

CHAPTER 11

·····

Inspiring the Humanistic (Jade) Thinker

·····

"When I look at the world I'm pessimistic, but when I look at people I am optimistic." - Carl Rogers (jade psychotherapist)

Vital Stats

Existential Level 6: Humanistic Thinking (Code: Jade)

Date of Origin: Approx. 1900 CE

Gravesian Theme: "Sacrifice self now in order to gain acceptance now."

Core Values: Equality, Honesty, Relatedness

Guiding Metaphor: Mankind is a family (and similar)

Goal: To find happiness in this life—in this moment—by relating deeply to other humans.

Representative Examples: Jimmy Carter, Michael Moore, New Agers John Lennon, Esalen Institute, group hugs, Jesus Christ (stereotypical portrayal), Eleanor Roosevelt, peace protesters, MLK's "I have a dream"

Basic Jade Credo

"Mankind is a family that we must heal by sacrificing our ego and being open. To make this family work, we must all embrace equality, honesty and relatedness."

General observations

The humanistic/jade mindset is a relatively new existential invention. In the United States, the mass emergence of this worldview happened most visibly during the 1960's civil rights, 'explore your inner self' 'free-love' era. Since this time, jade in our country has taken a decidedly more establishment-friendly pose. But core jade values remain unchanged. As always, jade embraces fairness, consensus and human relatedness.

From the vantage point of earlier thinking systems, jade thinking can appear dangerously naive. But don't be fooled. Jade is much more than a group hug—it is life's emerging attempt to solve the bitter divide within human consciousness itself. Without jade thinking, racism would still be tolerated and women would still be shunned in the workplace. Without jade thinking, no progressive political party could exist. Without jade thinking, the human spirit would surely shrivel and die.

Why did jade originate?

Like all new thinking systems, jade was born out of the new existential predicament caused by the successes of earlier systems. The copper commerce-based living sent our material quality of life skyrocketing to heights unknown in human history. Enterprising copper and disciplined navy thinking came together to make this success possible. They have also made it possible for many children of affluence to realize that worldly success doesn't make a person happy.

Jade flourishes when materialism loses its charm. Once a person determines that materialism is a futile path, his mind begins to search for a better way of experiencing joy and fulfillment in life. The fresh new joy that jade thinking offers relates to openness, intimacy, and trust—the thrill of inner connectedness with others.

Cynical copper thinking often ridicules this inner focus as weak or naive, but Martin Luther King's dream lives on in anyone willing to let their guard down long enough to imagine it. This is jade's dream for humanity. Unfortunately, this vision too often gets lost in jade's fuzzy maze of clichés, idealistic rhetoric, and self-congratulatory group-think. Like the messy-but-exuberant hippies of yesterday, jade thinkers of today face a daunting challenge of conveying their message in a way that doesn't cause nausea in the more hard-boiled 'worldly' types.

Core characteristics of jade

The core theme for the jade mindset is, "Sacrifice self now to gain acceptance now." This is a quantum evolution of the earlier navy mantra, "Sacrifice self now to attain future reward." Notice the similarity: both navy saintly thinkers and jade humanist thinkers are moved to sacrifice themselves to something bigger and more profound. The main difference is that jade thinkers don't want to wait until some hypothetical afterlife for their payoff. They want it now.

On the surface, jade thinkers can appear quite self-indulgent. They revel in the world of feelings. They see being connected with other humans as the ultimate purpose of human existence. A person newly inspired by jade-thinking seems to encounter the world with fresh eyes, with a jubilant sense that anything is possible through love. It is a refreshingly idealistic attitude towards life.

But, like most thinking systems, jade has a deep internal contradiction. Like navy absolutism, it can seem tremendously authoritarian and aggressive when cornered, becoming blinded by humanistic ideals in an embarrassingly hypocritical way. Imagine an angry, ranting jade thinker chastising innocent Christmas shoppers for buying clothes made in exploitative sweat shops, or showing pictures of mutilated animals to people chomping pork sandwiches at a BBQ stand. Not too humanistic, is it?

This is the paradox of jade. On one hand it embraces love as the apex of human existence, on the other hand it condemns those who dissent (although usually with more tact than indicated above). How can we reconcile these aspects of the jade character? We must see the hidden cause of all jade's angst—a gnawing sense of guilt for the very fact of existence. Remember copper? Copper was guiltless. Jade is the stage where all of that long-repressed copper guilt finally comes home to roost.

The jade mind lives in a perpetual state of guilt for the sufferings of mankind. It feels guilty for eating, guilty for working, guilty for not working, guilty for not being loving enough, guilty for everything. It does its best to assuage this guilt with idealistic aphorisms, but sometimes the love salve doesn't hold, causing involuntary eruptions of stabbing judgements, elitism and guilt trips for the rest of us.

But beneath all this guilt is an authentic love for mankind and a profound belief in the equality of all humans. The mucky existential lessons that jade thinkers must learn deal almost exclusively with intimacy and the non-reality of separation. These are not lessons for emotional cowards. That's why so many in our culture avoid the transformation (from copper to jade) with alcohol, sex, work and other addictions. Reality can be tough on vulnerable idealists and romantics. But growth cannot be avoided, and every bit of copper selfishness and navy righteousness must eventually be undone in the soft womb of jade humanism.

In the larger scheme, jade is doing what it must to heal the wounds of the past and prepare for a huge leap forward. After a long journey from scarcity and fear, the jade mind is finally starting to detach from the concept of separation so that it can truly be present, loving and peaceful.

Healthy jade: The gentle humanist

When they feel connected to others, jade thinkers are wonderful to be around. They are great listeners because—get this—they actually care! That's right. They care about you and everyone else in the room with genuine love and concern. Why? Because you are a human being. What better reason is there? Jade doesn't need a reason to care about others. To

---

Inspiration in action #24: Portrait of a jade artist

When jade values broke out in hives around the U.S. in the 1960's, the Beatles got swept up in the love-fest and turned from bubble-gum pop stars into sonic messengers of psychedelic humanism. In particular, John Lennon stands out still today as the poster-child for jade artistic thinking, with his paradoxically warm-but-rambunctious commitment to equality. If you want a crash course in the inner workings of the jade mind, buy Lennon's greatest hits album and listen to it thoroughly. "Imagine," "Power to the People," "Give Peace a Chance"…these songs speak with absolute clarity to the humanistic dreams that jade thinkers invariably cherish. (*Listener's note*: Psychedelics are always only optional.)

jade, reason is a cold and calculated invention of the human mind too often used as a barrier to keep truth at bay.

The healthy jade is a peaceful, unassuming sort. But don't mistake this for weakness. The healthy jade is simply upholding his principles by expressing his true, unguarded nature. Healthy jade is not looking for approval from others, as much as the opportunity to discover a mutuality with others. When this happens, an upward spiral of warmth kills the fear and anxiety, and the universe appears benevolent and majestic to all.

Unhealthy jade: the love junkie/egalitarian warrior

Have you ever met someone addicted to New-Age books and seminars? Unhealthy jade can take on a decidedly copper-like driven character in pursuit of inner peace. Like a greedy business person with money, unhealthy jade scarfs up every love opportunity that surfaces, but never quite feels satisfied. It is as if something inside the person cannot get through an invisible wall between the *concept* of love and love's direct *experience*. All manner of addictions may surface to compensate as the person moves farther and farther from center. The cycle escalates until the person dispenses with seeking altogether and lets the simple truth shine through: love, the animating source from within, cannot be found through trite cliches and external seeking.

In other unhealthy jade systems, we see a decidedly more navy-like tactic for dealing with jade guilt—militant activism. The most annoying know-it-alls populate this thinking dynamic, angrily spewing depressing but well-researched facts upon everyone within earshot. This is the jade version of absolutistic navy's 'fire and brimstone,' and it rarely wins any sane converts. Although this approach has a decidedly tough exterior, it operates from the same dynamic as the love-junkie—a frustrated urge to experience unconditional love and connection.

How does jade see America?

Jade often shows its patriotism in a way that confuses less complex systems: with criticism. Jade loves America, but often cannot always digest the bile that America's policy of global imperialism and corporate fascism produces in its gut. When it comes to old-school nationalistic dogmas, count jade out! The only dogmas that jades are prone to adopt are those that enforce kindness and tolerance for everyone. But as a uniquely patriotic member of society, jade does feel that it owes America the best it has to offer: clear, constructive feedback into the dangerous nature of free-market capitalism untempered by empathy and accountability.

At core, jade believes in people. At core, jade believes that truthful communication can solve all human problems. To fail to communicate is to fail one's fellow man, to fail one's world, to fail one's country. For jade, the means and the ends are one, and to lie in the name of a worthy cause is to betray the very values that sustain us. Jade feels this at a gut level, in the intuitive sense that something has gone drastically wrong with our country and in a faint (or severe) distaste for the status quo.

Many jade thinkers are so horrified by what they see when they look at our country that they'd rather tune out. They get discouraged and overwhelmed. Other courageous jade thinkers are determined to set the record straight and give America the corrective criticism that it requires. Outspoken media commentators like Michael Moore and Robert Greenwald represent patriotism in the healthiest shade of jade.

Inspiration in action #25: Portrait of a jade brand

Have you ever traveled on Southwest Airlines? Did you like it? When I ask people this question, I always get a strong response – positive, negative, or passionate ambivalence. It's a fascinating phenomenon that I was finally able to diagnose. Here goes: people feel towards Southwest the same way they feel towards jade thinkers in general. Why? Because Southwest airlines is a seamlessly jade company—from branding, to seating policies, to relaxed egalitarian corporate culture. Upon further research I discovered that this is not a coincidence. It just so happens that former Southwest Airlines CEO Howard Putnam actually consulted with Gravesian practitioner Dr. Don Beck to intentionally design nearly every aspect of Southwest's business in accordance with jade principles...Riddle solved!

How does jade see other thinking systems?

Jade thinkers try to love everyone but are often disappointed, vacillating between feelings of self-righteousness and victimhood when others fail to meet their lofty ideals.

JADE MEETS ABSOLUTISM/NAVY (LEVEL 4):

Jade often judges those who think in navy absolutes as mental dinosaurs, soon to go extinct. Jade sees all of the damage that blind obedience to authority has caused the world (holy wars, genocides, etc.) and wonders how people could be so stupid. However, when jade thinking is healthy and well-connected, it is able to accept and even embrace the fear that causes absolutist/navy thinking. Compassion is healthy jade's most profound strength. With navy, this strength is well served, and can unleash a powerfully purposeful partnership.

JADE MEETS INDIVIDUALISM/COPPER (LEVEL 5):

Jade is copper's most scathing critic. Remember, jade thinking actually emerged to compensate for the damage caused by copper's rampant individualism. As a result, jade is highly sensitive to copper's flaws—and all too eager to point them out. On the other hand, most jade thinkers are secretly envious of the intoxicating simplicity of copper's guiltless existence and often long to achieve the same material affluence and prestige. When jade thinkers resolve this ambivalence towards prosperity, they can become the happiest and most affluent members of our society. Successful jade gives copper an inspired foreshadowing of their potentially abundant, happy future.

JADE MEETS SYSTEMIC THINKING/GOLD (LEVEL 7):

Jade thinking usually finds itself both attracted and intimidated by gold thinking, because it integrates the warmth of jade humanity with the assertiveness of copper. Gold is able to fight without getting whiny, solve problems that defy logic, and communicate with people of every level (crimson, navy, copper, jade, etc.) without lying. Jade admires this, but doesn't always trust it. Problems also come when gold shows its individualistic roots and refuses to bow down to group norms. This disrupts jade's need for social harmony and consensus. Finally, jade often misinterprets gold's appreciation for individual differences as a form of elitism. Jade can be so committed to the ideology of equality that it confuses helpful pragmatic distinctions with value judgement—a dangerous (jade) perceptual bias that often causes more problems than it solves.

Who does jade trust?

Jade trusts in people who are willing to be vulnerable, and trusts in lofty ideals for mankind. But jade is highly mistrustful of (for profit) organizations and people who represent them. This cynicism stems from jade's observation of how people so often lose their deeper humanity in name of higher causes propagated by the powerful few to exploit the helpless many. The 'victim' myth is a huge part of jade's inner emotional mythology.

Beyond all ideology, in the here and now, jade thinkers are usually very warm and open to anyone who is authentic or "on the level." They are tremendously receptive to expressions of kindness and vulnerability. They want to give people the benefit of the doubt. They crave a sense of joy and connectedness in the here and now, and realize that trusting others is a huge part of living a good life.

When communicating with jade thinkers, it's helpful to represent yourself first and foremost as a human being. Jade thinkers feel that they deserve to be respected as fellow humans regardless of their background or accomplishments. To jade, true authority comes from authenticity and solidarity with others. More socially contrived forms of authority are usually deemed dubious, at best.

Tips for designing inspiring jade communications

Here are some general principles that I've found useful when designing communications intended to inspire humanistic/jade thinkers.

Step #1: Engage the Jade Sensory Filter:

As always, make sure to design your message with an aesthetic quality that resonates with the jade sensibilities of your audience. Jade generally prefers softness and relatability over glamour and glitz. Keep it warm, personable, and human. Jade thinkers are highly sensitive to the trappings of inauthenticity and mistrust tradition, so be careful when using antiquated designs from the past. Whatever you do, avoid carelessly adopting a mainstream corporate aesthetic, unless your communication purpose and context is particularly well-suited.

STEP #2: ENGAGE THE JADE MENTAL FILTER:

The jade mind is always scanning its environment for opportunities to feel good and connect. To get the jade mind working, you would be smart to get your audience to visualize pleasant humanity. Use words and images that evoke a sense of social warmth and community.

As always, situational framing is helpful. In what environment will the jade mind be experiencing this communication? Since jade is highly social, what are some aspects of community that relate to this particular environment? How can you tie your message into the immediacy of that specific social context? What are important others thinking or doing in that situation? Brainstorm your approach through the community context, or lens. If possible, integrate this into your design approach.

Value framing is always critical. How can you make your message demonstrate that you share jade's core values of equality, honesty and relatedness? Even better, how can your message also demonstrate that you understand jade's unique existential plight? In our copper-saturated culture, jade tends to feel alienated and disenfranchised. The jade mind is highly sensitive to being misunderstood. Why not reference your insight into this fact. A little compassion goes a long way. But don't fake it! Jade thinkers are smart, and they despise manipulation. This can work to your advantage if you deal with them as though they are intelligent, competent humans. If you truly respect them, you will earn their trust.

To create mental resonance, I sometimes find it helpful to employ jade's favorite metaphor—the human family. Traditional nuclear families don't always float jade's boat, as they too often mirror the despised dysfunctional patriarchal organizations. Instead, jade is moved by the global concept of family as embodied in the pop song "We are the World" (although not necessarily with that same goofy mid-80's aesthetic). The global family is a central organizing metaphor behind jade's proud vision. If you can authentically employ it to frame your message you will have a strong chance of engaging emotional rapport.

Besides the tactics given, feel free to draw from any number of the other mind-capturing strategies covered in Chapter 3 (*questioning, problem making personal recognition, storytelling,* etc.), catering these communication tactics to the humanistic values and aspirations of your audience.

STEP #3: OVERCOME THE JADE SPIRITUAL FILTER:

Once we've got the jade mind engaged, we can take it to the next level. In accordance with the principle of context, our design goal is now to help the person recontextualize their experience into something more expansive and pragmatic. We can do this by any combination of the approaches spelled out previously.

Jade thinkers are inspiration junkies, but they tend to be very sensitive to manipulation and guarded towards typical mass communication campaigns. The hardest part about inspiring jade is usually developing the trust needed to overcome their skepticism about your hidden motive. One great approach is to call out this skepticism directly and honestly. "If I were you, I'd probably be a bit skeptical right now..." (You get the idea.)

Distinguishing limiting metaphors can be helpful for encouraging jade thinkers to loosen their grip on current ways of seeing. The jade family metaphor is inspiring, but difficult to actualize. Sober, worldly eyes show mankind as a bloodthirsty family of bickering political parties, warring governments and self-serving capitalists. If you want to inspire your jade audience, you might start by gently encouraging them to look at the practical limitations of their current family metaphor in the face of the facts. Jade thinkers are usually open to this sort of inquiry, as long as it is framed as being in the service of something larger.

After establishing the limitations of the current metaphor, it can be helpful to invite the audience to consider trying out a more practical one:

Inspiration in Action #26: Portrait of two jade movies

Typical jade movies usually involve some sort of mid-to-late life existential crisis. The main character is a person who has found worldly success, but feels empty inside. For my money, the best examples invariably star actor Jack Nicholson. In "As Good as it Gets" (1997) and "About Schmidt" (2002) Nicholson plays a character who, despite financial security, is utterly incapable of relating to other human beings. The protagonist's emotional journey, in both cases, is to discover the importance of charity and compassion. In particular, the climax of "About Schmidt" stands for me as the most powerful and inspiring cinematic portrayal of humanity to ever grace the big screen. If you haven't seen it yet, please log onto www.netflix.com and have a copy sent to your home immediately. Your inner jade thinker will give you a big warm group hug.

---

life as a *system*. This will depersonalize things and bring a fresh planetary perspective, while still upholding the value of human equality and unity. This metaphor requires the individual change their mental center of gravity to emphasize pragmatism over ideology.

Invite your audience to consider looking at human life as one expression of something grander, a system in which all life participates. Urge them to see their role in the universe as support for this shared life. This idea will help jade thinkers retrieve a sense of purpose and agency (reminiscent of navy and copper thinking), but within a much larger playing field. The system metaphor solves the jade existential conundrum.

Another terrific, proven way to inspire jade is with a call to imagine. John Lennon's song "Imagine" and Martin Luther King's "I Have a Dream" speech are legendary examples of well-crafted calls to imagine. Such calls liberate the jade mind from the guilt of yesterday and the scarcity of today, creating a vivid, warm vision of future togetherness.

In our culture today, jade thinkers are considered the romantics and the idealists. What they sometimes lack in drive and worldly ambition, they more than make up for in noble emotion and sentiment. Don't inspire jade with fantastical, otherworldly dreams; make their dreams seem possible and imminent. The healthy jade has enough faith in humanity to believe that we can collectively accomplish anything we set our minds to. To jade, dreams are not fairy tales; they are impending realities.

When humanists transform into systemists...

Eventually jade begins to look around and notice that even humanism will not solve the problems that our species has created. The mind once again starts to loosen its grip. An explosive heart-longing pushes for a new expression, something universal and yet humble at the same time. When the idealism of humanism finally fades, the mind regenerates as a fresh new tool for living based upon a commitment to serving life on a planetary level (including, but not limited to, human beings).

As the gold system emerges from the chaos of jade's undoing, the individual has made a huge advancement, one that a relatively small percentage of humans on this planet have yet achieved. This person has escaped the orbit of survival, and reached the plane of thriving. With one foot now firmly planted in the formless realm behind the mind, gold thinking can now see both the forest and the trees. Fear dissipates, humor blossoms, and inspiration takes center stage.

Gold thinking holds the power to untangle all of the complex problems caused by humans operating from all earlier modes of being. To be a great communicator for the twenty-first century, a person must learn, understand, and operate from at least this level. Why? Because from this perspective it is easy to see that inspiration is nothing less than life energies in action, and that inspiring others is an imminently practical way to serve life's relentless push for growth.

CHAPTER 12

·····

INSPIRING THE SYSTEMIC (GOLD) THINKER

·····

"How wonderful that we have met with a paradox.
Now we have some hope of making progress."
- Niels Bohr (gold physicist)

Vital Stats

EXISTENTIAL LEVEL 7: Systemic Thinking (Code: Gold)

Date of Origin: Approx. 1950 CE (now emerging en masse)

Gravesian Theme: "Express self for what self desires and others need, but never at the expense of others, and in a manner that all life can continue to exist."

Core Values: Integrity, Competence, Sustainability

Guiding Metaphor: Life is a system (and similar)

Goal: To restore vitality and balance to a world torn asunder.

Representative Examples: "cultural creatives," Barack Obama, google, the sustainability movement, Clare Graves, David Bohm, Apple, collaborative innovation, readers of this book

Basic gold credo

"To serve life, I must express my own unique talents in a way that serves to uphold the health and evolution of all other systems in which I am embedded."

General observations

Mass emergence of the systemic/gold thinking system is the ongoing breakthrough of our times. This movement has been alternately pegged as a spiritual revolution, the sustainability movement, the LOHAS movement, and the rise of cultural creatives—to name just a few. Like branches from one tree, each of these movements has sprouted from the same underlying field of thinking and being. Graves first detected this field as it began to emerge in the early 1950's, but it is just now starting to take off, especially among Generation X'ers and those born after.

Before delving deeper into the characteristics of gold thinkers, it's important to make a couple of distinctions. First, we must always remind ourselves that gold (like all levels of existence) refers to a way of thinking, not to a type of person. Someone who habitually operates on the level of gold thinking may appear quite ordinary to the untrained eye. Also, please be aware that many humanistic/jade thinkers are now getting involved in the social movements pioneered by systemic/gold thinkers. The easiest way to distinguish between jade and gold thinkers is by their implied attitudes towards groups. Jade thinkers primarily join groups to feel good and be a part of something, while gold thinkers primarily join groups to contribute and help solve problems. As a result, gold thinkers are far less worried about emotional warmth and are far less concerned with finding group consensus. They want results.

At the end of the day, you'll find that communicating with gold audiences is invigorating if you're competent and terrifying if you're not. Gold thinkers are ruthlessly committed to serving life. They are not interested in wasting their own or anyone else's time. If you share this commitment, you will never find a more competent, creative, and inspiring group of human beings with whom to partner.

Why did gold originate?

Gold thinking was born out of the failures of all earlier survival-based modes of living. Navy saintly thinking emerged to create a sense of morality in a bloodthirsty (crimson) authoritarian world. But, in doing so, it created a sense of fear and repression that stifled the human expression. Copper individualism emerged to set the creative spirit free again. But, in so doing, it created a level of indiscriminate production that has polluted both the planet and our collective humanity. Jade humanism emerged to help us regain a sense of human connectedness, but has kept many addicted to feeling good and robbed them of their ability to discern and deal with genuine threats caused by people operating from unhealthy manifestations of earlier thinking systems (esp. crimson, navy and copper). Gold is life's new invention to help us remedy these shortcomings, and more.

We live in fascinating times. As our world spins kicking and screaming into this systemic new century, we see the rise and fall of every meaning system mankind has ever created. Jade's egalitarian victim's rights activism has unlocked copper's imperialistic grip on the third world. Copper's obsession with spreading capitalism and democracy has undermined the stabilizing navy theocracies that had before kept violent middle-east warlords contained. In our country, navy's obsession with imposing morality and copper's disdain for "big government" has blocked our government from initiating a more progressive, life serving agenda that might otherwise help to moderate this global chaos.

If it weren't for gold thinking, our species wouldn't have a snowball's chance of surviving! Gold is the first level of thinking that rises above ideology and truly observes the world without judgement. Fearless, gold pulls for the health of all levels and unblocks the system so that life—all life—can continue to spiral upward again.

Through the trials and tribulations of all earlier stages, gold thinkers have confronted all of the fears of existence—predators, an angry god, scarcity and loneliness—and have learned all are without essential merit. Leaving scarcity thinking behind, this person releases a tremendous burden of existential baggage and starts drawing directly from the infinite well of energies that emanate from the unifying causal realm.

Core characteristics of gold

The gold theme for living is "Express self for what self desires and others need, but never at the expense of others, and in a manner that all life can continue to exist." This requires that people express their individuality while still recognizing and respecting the individuality of others, an ontological balancing act of mind-boggling magnitude.

Think about it. To balance self-expression and empathy is to transcend the self/other illusion that characterizes all earlier survival-based levels of existence. To operate from gold is to fundamentally dispel the illusion of separation—at a visceral, gut level. Can you imagine the kind of leverage this insight might give a person?

The easiest way to identify those operating out of gold is by their vitality and their intrinsic commitment to life-serving goals. These people are not trying to look good, they are not trying to get rich, they are not trying to be moral people, they are not seeking approval. They are acting from a deep faith in life and a deep conviction in the value of the ends pursued. Would they mind being rich, looking good, and having everyone love them? No, probably not. But that sort of stuff is secondary. Life is the thing.

In the realm of communication and leadership, gold thinkers stand out for their uncanny ability to understand other people and raise them up to a higher vision. Healthy gold brings new vitality to whatever it touches. This is because gold minds truly grasp the importance of integrity, not as a moral concept, but as a structural necessity for the human (bio-psycho-social) system to operate effectively and achieve sustainable health.

Healthy gold: the uplifting problem solver

When they are feeling connected to their purpose and self-expressed, gold thinkers are frighteningly competent and prolific. They have an unflappable sense of self-assurance mixed with a genuine care and empathy for others. They are endlessly creative and can adapt to any situation to bring about the best possible end-result. They are socially flexible and willing to be both leader or follower as the situation (and their abilities) dictate. Because they have defined their personal role in terms of contribution, they are able to bring about success for themselves and others without compromising the bottom line.

Unhealthy gold: the explosive know-it-all

If a gold thinker gets frustrated by your incompetence, you should probably run for the hills. Gold's commitment to life can take a decidedly arrogant form at times (resembling earlier copper/crimson egocentrism). The problem is that gold thinkers can get so caught up in their commitments that they lose patience for the rest of us.

It's an interesting conundrum. At most earlier levels of thinking, the individual's behavior is kept in check by a 'healthy' level of fear. Gold thinkers have less fear and may let themselves be quite explosive and primal at times. To understand these outbursts, one must realize that gold thinkers are always seeking a way to balance personal self-expression with concern for others. Being human, they fail. Their passions get misdirected, and they attack you as if you are the source of life's imbalance. Give them a little space. They'll come around.

How does gold see America?

Gold sees America as a promising, evolving system. It sees areas of health and disease that plague our social systems, usually understanding these as symbols of the broader human planetary condition. Gold is the system that generates creative solutions to our national problems and fearlessly challenges authority whenever necessary in an effort to resolve the blockages that keep our upward evolution in check.

Inspiration in Action #27: Portrait of a gold tycoon

Gold thinkers are like chameleons. One minute they might be dressed up in a tuxedo accepting an award, the next minute they might be clad in scruffy overalls participating in a hog-calling competition. But one common denominator among gold thinkers is that they are highly competent at what they do. A great example is Virgin founder Richard Branson. This ordinary man has managed to create a brand empire that prospers in almost every industry, while still finding personal time to create a commercial space program, fund alternative energy research, and take frequent failed hot air balloon journeys around the globe. Branson's infectious joy and demeanor is the sign of someone who is highly committed to life, but who doesn't actually take it—or himself—all that seriously. This is how healthy gold thinkers engage life. We should all be so lucky (and one day, I'm sure we will).

The gold brand of patriotism is not a "love it or leave it" proposition, but rather a visionary experiment to push boundaries of possibility. It transcends party lines (although it typically wears the mask of a 'progressive' or an 'independent') and seeks mainly to rally the country around unifying goals. It asks that Americans take responsibility for our actions and come together as a symbol to the rest of humanity of what the human spirit can accomplish when energized by an honest respect for life.

How does gold see other thinking systems?

Gold is the first thinking system with a clear insight into the unique strengths and limitations of the other existential levels. Instead of judging, fighting, or seeking to control others, healthy gold does what it can to pull for the healthy expression of other systems.

GOLD MEETS ABSOLUTISM/NAVY (LEVEL 4):

On a gut level, gold thinkers often find fundamentalist navy thinkers to be frustratingly simple-minded. But healthy gold also admires and respects the clarity of navy's deep conviction and purpose. Instead of challenging navy's fear-based need for clear authority, more skillful gold seeks to help navy channel their strengths towards worthy life-serving goals. But if the navy thinker isn't willing to play along, don't expect them to waste a whole lot of time fretting about it.

Inspiration in Action #28: Portrait of a gold brand

Have you ever wondered why Apple's products are so popular despite their insanely high prices? It's because, being a highly gold company, Apple builds innovation into the DNA of nearly every single product. The *iPod, iTunes*, the *iPhone*…these products did not come from a mind that was trying merely to play it safe and make ends meet. These products are bold and innovative. While traditional technology products seem to start with an established idea and seek to improve upon it, Apple products seem to start with raw vision and then work backwards to implement it. This is precisely how gold creative types think—from bold possibility to practical reality. The moral of the story? Not only is inspiration fun, but it comes with jaw-dropping business perks and incentives.

GOLD MEETS INDIVIDUALISM/COPPER (LEVEL 5):

Gold intuits the strengths and weaknesses of copper individualism very clearly. Both are expressive systems; both are passionately committed to their goals. The major difference is that gold has been humbled by jade humanism and purged of much of that repressed, copper guilt. Healthy gold respects copper industriousness and realizes that the solution to copper selfishness is not to pile on more guilt. On the contrary, pragmatic gold seeks to harness copper's industrious energies towards the solution of the very problems created by copper's industries. Gold thinkers with a penchant for communication are experts at inspiring copper thinking towards a more uplifting agenda.

GOLD MEETS HUMANISTIC/JADE (LEVEL 6):

Gold and jade are like a smart-but-nattering young married couple. Gold has insight into the narcissism of jade's feeling-centered approach to life, but also appreciates the value of jade's humanistic ideals. Because gold innovations often have an inspiring essence, jade loves to jump on the bandwagon and become an advocate for gold causes. This generally helps both parties and the whole of humanity—as long as gold leaders can manage to keep the movements from devolving into self-congratulatory love-fests. (*Note*: this is an evolutionary upgrade of the fabled copper/navy dyad that built the United States, and the gold/jade dyad will likely become the dominant force in recreating our country during the 21st century.)

Who does gold trust?

Gold trusts in life itself and its own intuitive assessments of other people. Gold is not seeking social approval (like jade), personal advantage (like copper) or a sense of absolute truth (like navy). Gold is not seeking anything but an opportunity to contribute. As a result, gold thinkers have a boundless sense of self-confidence and are usually great judges of character. Their faith in life is such that, even when they screw up, they always come away with a valuable lesson. So why worry?

As a default strategy, gold chooses trust. Does this mean that gold can be easily taken advantage of? Not for a minute. Gold can smell inauthenticity a mile away and usually steers clear of people with unsavory motives. The gold mind realizes that all trust is ultimately self-trust, and chooses friends and life situations according to its own instincts. This lack of fear and defensiveness gives it an uncommon level of charisma with which to attract talented, trustworthy friends and business associates.

Tips for designing inspiring gold communications...
Although every situation is unique, here are some principles that I've found useful when designing media and communications that inspire gold thinkers:

STEP #1: ENGAGE THE GOLD SENSORY FILTER:
As always, make sure to design your message with an aesthetic quality that resonates with the gold sensibilities of your audience. With gold the idea or concept behind the design may stand out more than the actual content. Gold can appreciate a wide range of styles. In general, a simple, classy, uncluttered presentation works best. Playfulness and visual irony can be great, but avoid being unnecessarily complicated or pretentious. Quality, elegance and authenticity are paramount.

STEP #2: ENGAGE THE GOLD MENTAL FILTER:
The gold mind is always scanning for vitality, and for good ideas waiting to happen. The best way to get gold's attention is by demonstrating competence and integrity in your work. It is also important that the content of what you are communicating be relevant to the particular goals of your gold audience.

It's hard to be overly specific here. Gold thinkers are so complex and diverse that you must really know your gold audience before choosing an approach. Is your audience composed of gold business executives? Environmentalists? Software designers? Politicians? Social activists? Filmmakers? Whoever they are, think about the world from their perspective and imagine what challenges they might typically face. Cater your communication to speak directly to those challenges and to the *systemic implications* that these challenges may create for them. This is a sophisticated form of situational framing that works well with gold thinkers. It demonstrates competence (a key attention grabber for gold minds).

Value framing is always a trusted ally. Use words and questions that evoke in gold a sense of genuine quality and commitment to the core gold values (integrity, competence, sustainability). But don't just paste these words on as an afterthought. Be authentic. Gold gets annoyed by the opportunistic commercialization of gold initiatives by copper capitalists and jade joiners. If you want to be taken seriously, it wouldn't hurt to gracefully distinguish yourself from the bandwagon by demonstrating your genuine commitment to gold causes and your appreciation for fearless self-expression. At the end of the day, you want to make sure the gold audience knows that you understand its unique existential plight and that you are in the game for the right reasons, like they are.

Communicator beware: Gold thinkers have great instincts and can sense when aesthetics and message are out of sync. More than any other level, they are perceptive to the context in which communication occurs. This is why simple, high concept, efficient designs tend to resonate so well—they demonstrate an understanding of the fundamental nature of context, and let the light shine through unabated.

The guiding metaphor for gold is the idea of life as a system. Win over the gold mind by gracefully employing the systems metaphor. Better yet, *demonstrate* your understanding of systems in the way you communicate complex ideas with simple visuals and language. If appropriate, show how other metaphors applied to the same situation can create fundamentally different outcomes. Gold thinking tries on different worldviews like tourists try on cheap sunglasses.

Besides the tactics given, feel free to draw from any number of the other mind capturing strategies covered in Chapter 3 (*questioning,*

Inspiration in Action #29: Portrait of a gold film

In 1999 director Sam Mendes and writer Alan Ball teamed up to create one of the most thematically sophisticated films ever to achieve both mass popularity and critical acclaim. At first blush, "American Beauty" might seem like just another mid-life crisis movie about the perils of materialism. But closer inspection shows that this film is actually about something much more mind-blowing—the paradox of life beyond form and the unreality of separation. The key to the film is the point of view of the narrator (played by actor Kevin Spacey). He speaks from beyond the grave, telling the story of his own imminent demise. This creates a context in which the viewer engages the film world from a viewpoint that is somehow beyond the physical world, and yet still embedded in the drama of existence. But this is really just the tip of the thematic iceberg for a film that—much like a gold thinker—defies established categories and conventions, yet still somehow makes simple ordinary sense.

---

problem making personal recognition, storytelling, etc). The important thing is that you cater these communication tactics to the particularly innovative, life serving values and aspirations of your systemic/gold thinking audience.

STEP #3: OVERCOME THE GOLD SPIRITUAL FILTER:
Once we've got the gold mind engaged, we can take it to the next level. In accordance with the principle of context, our design goal is now to help gold minds recontextualize their experience into something more expansive. We can do this by any combination of the tactics outlined in Chapter 3, especially the calls (imagine, action and duty) and the use of transformational metaphors (e.g. life as a dream).

Having already purged their spiritual filter of much fear and guilt, gold thinkers are not difficult to inspire once you've earned their trust. As a rule, gold thinkers are generally inspired and inspiring. In fact, most gold thinkers (consciously or unconsciously) use their own level of inspiration as an internal compass for determining whether or not you are being authentic. Having grown accustomed to feeling invigorated and abundant, gold thinkers view energy lapses as a sign that they are in the wrong environment, or have somehow fallen out of integrity.

All you can really do to open the gold spiritual filter is to make sure you don't accidentally shut it down by being manipulative or irrelevant! In other words, you must be authentic, produce quality work, and design your communication with a deep respect for gold values. This is not to say that gold is beyond transformation—no one is ever beyond transformation. But to a system that makes its own decisions and no longer feels motivated by fear, the push for transformation will come when the thinker is good and ready and not a minute sooner.

When systemists transform into mystics...

According to Graves research, gold systemic thinkers eventually turn from an outward focus on solving worldly problems to an inward focus on intuition and the holistic conception of reality. The gold mind surrenders to the fact that problems will never really be solved, and perhaps wonders what it might be like to experience a world without the last bit of ego self that keeps it feeling still separate.

With this final great surrender, the gold brain seems to shift from a left-hemisphere dominated problem-solving mode to right-hemisphere dominated holistic experiential mode. When this happens, the world turns from problem to poem, and gold thinking has cooled into indigo.

Thinking at this final holistic level of human existence bears uncanny resemblance to the thinking of great mystics, artists, and spiritual leaders throughout the ages. A poetic, intuitive sense of oneness with all that is perfumes the indigo experience in a way that defies rational explanation. Grandeur and mystery radiate from even the most mundane details of living. Life as a system transforms into life as a dream.

At this point in history, indigo thinkers make up only a small portion of the human population. Time will tell us what lessons they will have to teach, and what amazing new ways of experiencing life will emerge once indigo thinking has finally run its course.

CHAPTER 13

.....

INSPIRING MIXED AUDIENCES

.....

"First you harmonize, then you customize." - Wilson Pickett

Like any art, becoming inspirational requires practice. The great news is that this practice mustn't feel like you're getting a tooth pulled—it happens effortlessly once you've established the correct mental software, or map. The hardest part is getting the map 'installed.' The rest happens through spontaneous insight, and inspiration itself.

So far, for learning purposes, we have been basically assuming that all audiences (and people) are homogeneous mixtures of folks inhabiting the same rung of the existential ladder. Sometimes this is true, but usually it isn't. In the real world, at any given time, we are likely to find a scaled mixture of thinking types within the same group and within the same person over time. This is how it should be. According to Graves, each of these earlier thinking capacities is hard-wired into our very nervous system. As we evolve, the strengths and lessons of earlier existential levels remain always at our disposal.

What does this mean for us as inspirational communicators? It means that once we get a feel for the basic notes on the musical scale of human existence, we can then learn to play these notes in ornate melodies that move people and audiences of every mixture and type, through media of all forms, in situations of varying levels of complexity. Learning this level of mastery takes time, but the rewards are life-long. We won't be able to cover every advanced application in this one modest manual, but will at least give you some broad principles and a taste of what lies ahead.

Grasping the four bottom lines

To simplify the application of the Gravesian framework, I've found it helpful to think of each existential level as corresponding to a specific neurological system within each person that we seek to activate through words, sounds and symbols. As complex as the Gravesian lens may at first appear, understand that we are almost always dealing with just the following four fundamental components of meaning, or bottom lines: purpose, profit, people, and planet.[10] The four dominant existential levels covered earlier correlate with these four bottom lines as follows:

Navy serves Purpose

Absolutistic/navy values correspond with that part of our nervous system that responds to the idea of a clear transcendent purpose for living. Words, sounds and images that evoke a sense of absolute purpose activate this aspect of our experiential capacity.

Copper serves Profit

Individualistic/copper values seem to correspond with that part of our nervous system that responds to the idea of profit, or personal gain. Words, sounds and images that evoke a sense of personal advantage activate this aspect of our experiential capacity.

Jade serves People

Humanistic/jade values seem to correspond with that part of our nervous system that responds to a sense of human relatedness. Words, sounds and images that evoke a sense of human love and community activate this aspect of our experiential capacity.

Gold serves Planet

The systemic/gold values seem to correspond with that part of our nervous system that responds to the idea of serving life. Words, sounds and images that evoke a sense of planetary sustainability and health activate this aspect of our experiential capacity.

Audiences are more or less sensitive to a particular bottom line depending upon their preferred thinking style. Navy audiences emphasize transcendent purpose, copper audiences emphasize profit, jade audiences emphasize people and relatedness, while gold audiences emphasize planetary and systemic solutions. The more complex and diverse your audience, the

---

Inspiration in Action #30: The birth of planetary perspective

If an ordinary picture is worth a thousand words, then the picture taken by astronaut Bill Anders on Christmas Eve, 1968 officially left the world speechless. After a year of deep national and civil conflict, the nation was gifted on this particular day with a lonely shot of earth, taken from the moon, spinning silently as the sun spread across it's waking face. This was the first time humans had ever seen our earth from this perspective. The social impact was awesome. Titled "Earthrise" this photograph has been heralded by some as the birth of modern environmentalism and the rise of mass planetary thinking. This credit may or may not be deserved, but one thing is certain: viewing our planet from space lends a whole new perspective to our petty little human squabbles.

---

more helpful it can be to integrate multiple bottom lines into your visual design and messaging. This will help you uplift target audiences (and specific individuals) with complex and diverse thinking styles, without falling into the trap of pandering or being generic.

Merging bottom lines with scaled messaging

One way to integrate bottom lines so that you can reach mixed audiences is with an approach I call *scaled messaging*. This process allows us to shift our audience's perceptual context by guiding them up to a higher (more complex) bottom line or bring them down to a lower (less complex) one, to suit our communication purposes.

How does it work? Basically scaled messaging involves leading the listener through a series of targeted questions, comments, and topics intended to hit at each of these bottom lines (planet, people, profit and purpose) in seamless, rhythmic succession.

To illustrate in a simplified generic way, let's imagine that we are tasked with writing a commercial that inspires a generic national audience to purchase a high-quality environmentally friendly product. If we assume that our audience has an even distribution of all four dominant thinking types, we might write ad copy along these lines: "You care about the health of our planet. If you were able, wouldn't you do whatever you could to help fix the environmental crisis before it gets out of hand? [*targets gold/planet*] In doing so, wouldn't it be nice to feel that sense of fulfillment that comes from a shared purpose with others in your community? [*targets jade/people*] On a more personal level, aren't you tired of wasting precious money and energy that could be used to help you and your family get ahead? [*targets copper/profit*] Let's face it, at the end of the day, don't you just want to do the right thing? [*targets navy/ purpose*] Well, here's the good news: You don't have to choose..."

You get the idea. We started with the most lofty bottom line and brought it down to the most essential, hitting every bottom line along the way. Not everyone shares a conscious interest in the welfare of the planet, or even in being connected to others, but almost everyone does care about personal gain and providing for their family's future. By combining all four bottom lines into one succinct pitch, we were able to take everyone (except for sociopaths) down to a level of common need. Our next step would be to artfully demonstrate how our product meets those needs.

Please note that this exact same procedure can be used in reverse—to call people up to the highest bottom line. To do this we would just switch the order of our appeals. This might show up as follows: "You care about your children. Don't you want to do the right thing for them? [*targets purpose*] And wouldn't it be great if, in doing so, you could also save money and win a better quality of life? [*targets profit*] In fact, what if it was possible to do all of this while also feeling that ineffable sense of joy that comes from connecting with others while doing something positive for the world? [*targets people and planet*] Well, good news: You don't need to be cynical. The time has come when you really can have all of these things..."

This upward message scaling can have a particularly strong impact if done authentically. Try it and see. The reason for this is simple—we have invited our audience to experience a more expansive worldview by first creating a sense of safety and then calling them upwards. With this approach, we've included everyone's favorite bottom line and called everyone to a grander vision. You'll notice that many successful ad campaigns over the years have intuitively employed a similar approach. The difference is that now we have a scientific model that spells out exactly how and why it works. This gives us the ability to be even more precise in forming and sequencing our ideas to create maximum impact.

Narrowing the problem space

In practice, we can usually narrow our messaging to just one or two bottom lines. This process will drive naturally from the context in which our communication occurs. Typically, either the product we're selling or the communication medium itself will dictate a certain direction for emphasis. Limiting our scope can help us develop messages that are much more sophisticated and compelling.

For example, in keeping with our environmental theme, let's imagine that we are speaking to a somewhat skeptical corporate audience in order to motivate a sales division to get on-board with a new jade product. In this audience, we can generally assume a strong copper individualistic orientation with a shade of jade humanism. As a result, we can assume that your audience members are primarily interested in achieving personal goals, but strive to be ethical and sometimes feel guilty for putting self above others, and have occasional bouts of work-induced loneliness. They are all working hard, probably dreaming of an early retirement where they can relax and sip margaritas while writing the great American novel. How might we use scaled messaging to inspire this group?

We could first appeal to their need for personal profit. Make it acceptable to seek personal gain. Regale individualistic values. Once we've done this, we will have helped the audience alleviate the unconscious sense of guilt that they feel for being so self-directed (trust me, they might not freely admit or be aware of it, but the vast majority of these folks have been repressing a gnawing sense of guilt for many years). After we've got them relaxed and feeling accepted, we might then gracefully call upon them to reconsider their own profit orientation through the lens of a higher bottom line (either people or the planet).

Thinking Type	Credo	Preferred Bottom Line
Navy Absolutistic (Level 4)	*Life is a test in which I must prove myself worthy by sacrificing my own desires and delaying immediate gratification. To accomplish this I must uphold absolute, properly sanctioned laws.*	Purpose
Copper Individualistic (Level 5)	*Life is a competitive game in which I must achieve my goals in whatever way I can without getting into trouble. To win I must truly understand the value of personal power.*	Profit
Jade Humanistic (Level 6)	*Mankind is a family that we must heal by sacrificing our ego and being open. To make the family work we must truly embrace equality, honesty and relatedness.*	People
Gold Systemic (Level 7)	*To serve life, I must express my own unique talents in a way that serves to uphold the health and evolution of all other systems in which I am embedded.*	Planet

For example, using our hypothetical product as a tool, we might show how planetary service can lead not only to great profits, but also to a sense of fulfillment that transcends money. We might tell a story that calls this audience (through vicarious experience) to switch from a game metaphor (copper) to a systems metaphor (gold). This new metaphor would help them resolve the experiential dichotomy between self and other that keeps them emotionally defensive. If we've earned their trust before trying this, they will emotionally identify with the new metaphor, creating a profound sense of inner expansion.

Resonant Metaphor	Transformational Metaphor
Life is a *test*	Life is a *game*
Life is a *game*, world is a *machine*,	Mankind is a *family*
Mankind is a *family*	Life is a *system*
Life is a *system*	Life is a *dream*

Perhaps our closing comments would sound like this: "What if this isn't just a bunch of spin? Imagine for a minute that you could actually win at the business game—make lots of money, take care of your family, have nice things, and all that—while still feeling connected to others and serving the planet. Does this sound like a fairy tale? Well, it isn't. Not anymore. This is the emerging reality for today's business leaders. To avoid becoming an outdated relic of the 20th century, consider looking at life not as a winner-take-all game, but as a game in which the only real winners are the ones who make a choice to help the planet prosper. This is your new mission and, in my opinion, our new product is your best chance for achieving it. Listen, I do realize that you are a grown-up. You will make up your own mind. But as grown-ups, we have to be willing to ask the tough questions in order to move forward. Here's a tough question for you to consider: are you willing to suspend your cynicism and see a life-changing opportunity when it comes your way? It's your life. Do with it whatever you choose. But I invite you to see this as an amazing opportunity and to take action now. Right now—on behalf of yourself, your children and the planet that they'll soon inherit."

Do you think the copper/jade audience will be inspired? Assuming that we are being authentic and that we've used framing tools to first cultivate a deep sense of personal relevance before making our close—absolutely, yes! Why? Because we've spoken to their existing bottom line (profit) while calling them to embrace a larger one (planet). This will unconsciously liberate them from the feeling of separation and show them a better way. This is exactly what Martin Luther King, Jr. and John F. Kennedy did to become visionary leaders of their generation, and it is what you will do to become a visionary leader of yours. But first, you must fully grasp, practice and apply the basics.

I've used these strategies to create many moving speeches, in many different contexts, for many years, but feel that I am still only beginning to grasp and apply the power of this approach. To expedite your particular learning path, please refer to the table on the previous page. It gives an overview of the important information covered in the past few chapters on the four dominant thinking systems as they relate to scaled messaging. These are indeed the notes and scales that you must learn in order to spontaneously improvise on the instrument of human inspiration.

Means vs. Core values

As your understanding of this framework matures, your ability to understand the way people make sense of the world will grow in ways that defy your current imagination. Grasping people's thinking level, core values and preferred bottom line is only the first step. The next step involves observing the preferred methods, or means, through which people express and realize these values. In most people, means and ends are often distinct.

For example, humanistic/jade thinkers prize humanity and connection above all else. These core aspirations form the basis for their deepest convictions about what the world should be and represent noble goals that they hope to bring to fruition. But this knowledge tells us little or nothing about how they typically go about trying to achieve these goals. One person might strive to create a sense of connection and humanity by sharing feelings and being open. Another might find it best to be more guarded and strategic in their communications. Yet another might feel that righteous ranting is the best way to wake people from their slumber.

How can we learn to see the similarity of shared core values across people with vastly different ways of expressing them? Fortunately, our framework can help to simplify this process greatly. In addition to spelling out the eight different aspirational goals of mankind, the Gravesian levels also represent eight distinct approaches or "means" that people typically use to accomplish their goals, as follows:

LEVEL 1: *Autistic/Tan*
People who adopt autistic/tan means use apathy and indulgence as a way to accomplish their goals. Stereotypical examples: extreme food addiction, the lethargic unemployed and unmotivated welfare recipients.

LEVEL 2: *Magical Tribal/Violet*
People who adopt violet means use magic to accomplish their goals. Stereotypical examples: snake charmers, superstitious people, performers of rites and incantations.

LEVEL 3: *Warrior/Crimson*
People who adopt crimson means use aggression and force to accomplish their goals. Stereotypical examples: thugs, dictators, mobsters and *The Jerry Springer Show* guests.

LEVEL 4: *Absolutistic/Navy*

People who adopt navy means use absolute rules and regulations to accomplish their goals. Stereotypical examples: the clergy (priests and nuns), soldiers, police officers and strict parents.

LEVEL 5: *Individualistic/Copper*

People who adopt copper means use strategy and tactics to accomplish their goals. Stereotypical examples: politicians, research scientists, salesmen and engineers.

LEVEL 6: *Humanistic/Jade*

People who adopt jade means use dialogue and feelings to accomplish their goals. Stereotypical examples: 12-step program attendees, encounter groups, liberals and hippies.

LEVEL 7: *Systemic/Gold*

People who adopt gold means use inspiration and insight to accomplish their goals. Stereotypical examples: inventors, theoretical physicists, creative artists and great performers.

LEVEL 8: *Holistic/Indigo*

People who adopt indigo means use humility and surrender to accomplish their goals. Stereotypical examples: mystics, saints and world spiritual leaders.

Although I provided stereotypical examples, please understand that each of the above levels can, in theory, be used as a means towards accomplishing any ends whatsoever. For example, it is quite possible that a person with the relatively advanced end values of gold could occasionally adopt primal crimson tactics for accomplishing their planetary goals. We might call someone like this an "illusion destroyer"—someone who lovingly uses confrontational or provocative means to shake people out of their slumber and help them embrace an urgent truth.

As a general rule, I've observed that a person's habitual communication means type falls at the same or lower level of complexity than their core thinking style. For example, it is far more likely to see someone with humanistic/jade values expressing their ideals in an all-or-nothing absolutistic/navy way than to see someone with individualistic/copper core values approaching a frustrated goal with holistic/indigo humility and surrender. Is it impossible for someone to adopt habitual 'means' values more sophisticated than their habitual 'end' values? Sure, why not. It's just not something I've often witnessed, except in times of profound crisis (such as on 9/11/2001 in New York City) when a person is forced by circumstances to transcend habitual modes of thinking and rise to the occasion.

At the end of the day, understanding the difference between 'means' and 'ends' values will give you communication leverage in at least two ways. First, it will make you better able to listen and stop confusing people's communication style with their conversational goals. This will give you tremendous insight into other people's buried intentions—good, bad or otherwise. Second, as a communicator (speaker, media designer, etc.) it will give you greater freedom to choose a communication style or persona that resonates with your target audience.

A more thorough discussion of this exciting topic must wait until a future volume. Nonetheless, we will conclude this section by teasing you with a taxonomy of the specific means and ends value combinations that you'll most commonly find roaming the U. S. today. If we assume that most American citizens fall into one of the four major thinking types (navy, copper, jade, and gold), and if we cut off the tail-end of the distribution for means types (eliminating tan and indigo), we can generate a matrix of eighteen different means/ends combinations. These combinations represent eighteen specific communication styles or personas, many of which you may recognize from characters in your own life, on television, in books and in film.

Please look over the table on the next page. As you do so ask yourself: Which communication persona do I most often adopt? Which one would I like to use more frequently? Where do my pop-culture heroes and villains fit onto this list? Which personas has this book been using to inspire me thus far? (*Hint:* there are three and they are on the top row.)

	Gold Means (insight)	Jade Means (dialogue)	Copper Means (strategy)
Gold Ends (sustainability)	The Benevolent Visionary	The Inspirational Communicator	The Benevolent Entrepreneur
Jade Ends (humanity)		The Consensus Builder	The Calculating Humanist
Copper Ends (individuality)			The Bootstraps Individualist
Navy Ends (morality)			

Remember: Inspiration is an art

If the information that we've covered so far seems to you a bit overwhelming in terms of scope and creative possibilities, then I'm pleased to hear it. This means you're starting to get a broader vision for just how profound and revolutionary this framework can be for those who are willing to engage it. But, whatever you do, please know that inspiring others is not a chore, nor is it a duty—it is an honor and an exquisite art.

Becoming a great artist is hard work, but it is also fun. Great art has an immeasurably powerful impact on the world, but is usually created for its own sake, rather than for the sake of some hidden ulterior motive. Great art blurs the lines between work and play by tapping into an infinite realm that we all share and reflecting this realm so that others can experience the depths of their own hidden creative potential. Great art evokes a sense of gratitude and soul-longing that effortlessly silences the strategic, critical, life-choking mind.

Navy Means (sacrifice)	Crimson Means (force)	Violet Means (magic)
The Painful Truth Teller	The Illusion Destroyer	The Practical Shaman
The Militant Egalitarian	The Victim Protector	The Metaphysical Explorer
The Pious Opportunist	The Ruthless Capitalist	The Mesmerizing Salesman
The Hardboiled Fundamentalist	The Righteous Warrior	The Snake Charmer

The simple, timeless painting that somehow inspires the masses for centuries inside a museum may have been painted quickly, but the raw artistic genius that underlies it was refined through years of painstaking labor and humble dedication to the craft. Should the craft of designing timeless, inspiring communications be any different?

Allow yourself to enjoy the process of becoming a transformational communicator. You now have all of the basic information that you'll need. From this point forward, trial and error in a spirit of playful exploration will be the quickest path to mastery.

Part III.

THE PRACTICE: Applying Transformational Design ™

In Part III we'll offically unveil the Transformational Design® spiral — a simple, highly practical blueprint for social change. We'll also outline a five-step design process that can be used to guide absolutely any communication design endeavor from start to finish. Finally, we'll envision how these tools might be used to help us craft a more joyful personal and planetary future.

 ← "WHAT" IS HERE

CHAPTER 14

·····

PUTTING IT ALL TOGETHER

·····

"Nothing is quite so practical as a good theory."
– Kurt Lewin

In the introduction, we proposed that our currently accepted maps of human nature are outdated, causing at least three major inspiration-killing communication tactics: the *Shallow Human* fallacy in which we deny the spiritual nature of our audience, the *People-Are* fallacy in which we unconsciously project our values onto others, and the *Scarcity* fallacy in which we propagate the notion that there's not enough to go around for everyone. The entire book, up to this point, has been engineered to systematically undo these three deadly assumptions and replace them with something more practical and uplifting.

In Part I we used the dimensional model to demonstrate that people are complex, multi-dimensional beings with a shared spiritual essence. We redefined communication along these lines and suggested that the whole idea of 'scarcity' is based on the misguided notion that we are primarily physical beings struggling for survival in a random, chaotic universe. We noted that genuinely inspirational communication stems from authenticity ("self as source") and from the skillful application of design principles, to help our audience overcome barriers to the experience of their own innate spiritual essence.

In Part II we applied the research of psychologist Clare W. Graves to clarify the vastly different ways that people make sense of the world. We saw that, even though all humans derive inspiration from the same underlying source, their minds represent this source according to hidden value systems that make their perceptions of reality quite distinct. We argued that in order to communicate effectively with an audience, we must understand and respect the way they make sense of the world around them, and frame our message to fit their preexisting worldviews.

We are now ready to put all of these big ideas together and unveil our spanking new Transformational Design map. Exciting, isn't it?

Good design = harnessing unseen forces

Inspirational communication pulls for the recipient to experience eternal, spiritual truth. It works with the principles of mental evolution by acknowledging and harnessing unseen forces for the upward movement and outward expansion of life. Good communication design happens effortlessly once we start asking the right questions and are willing to trust fully in the answers that inspiration itself delivers.

When we take all of the fancy language out of the way, we find that the art of communication is both intentional and tactical. Authentic intentions come naturally from an acknowledgment of our spiritual connection to others. From this authentic starting point, we can then effortlessly apply the mental tactic of empathy to leverage messages that hit people where they live. The knowledge required to become an inspirational communicator is not complex. It's based on the answers to two simple, game-changing questions.

Important question #1: How are all people alike?

Answer: All humans are multi-dimensional beings. Body, mind, and spirit come together in myriad ways to produce people of infinite, varying forms, but always sharing one fundamental essence. Inspiration is the experience that occurs when one accesses this essence. A message/stimulus must travel a particular path in order to inspire. It must pass through a series of experiential thresholds, or filters. These are:

1. THE SENSORY FILTER: the stimulus must stand out and capture our audience's senses.

2. THE MENTAL FILTER: the stimulus must generate interest and get our audience thinking.

3. THE SPIRITUAL FILTER: stimulus must move our audience to momentarily disidentify with the mind and be present.

These three thresholds respond to different dimensions or characteristics of our message, ranging from aesthetics (sensory filter) to personal relevance (mental filter) to authenticity and context (spiritual filter). An expert communicator leverages these design principles to craft messages that forge a context in which all audience filters are spontaneously overcome, and inspiration naturally emerges. The specific filter-related design goals and tactics are spelled out below.

Filter	Design Goal	Engagement Tactics
Sensory (WHAT)	Capture Attention	surprise, aesthetics, sensory design (visual, auditory, kinesthetic, etc.), media type, media placement
Mental (HOW)	Generate Interest	situation framing, personal recognition, value framing, questioning, problem making, storytelling, resonant metaphors
Spiritual (WHY)	Transcend Thinking	authenticity, humor, listening, unspoken truths, demonstrating trust, repetition and rhyme, story payoffs, solutions, limiting metaphors, transformational metaphors, calls to duty, calls to action, calls to imagine, silence

Important question #2: How do people differ meaningfully?

Answer: Humans differ in the way they use their minds to pattern the material world. These differences derive from different values, life themes, and core metaphors. Minds exist on a continuum of mental complexity. There are eight distinct thinking types, or levels of existence.

EXISTENTIAL LEVEL 1: *Autistic Thinking*

Theme: Express self as an animal according to the dictates of urgent physiological needs.

Life Goal: Find sustenance (food, water, sex) and satisfy biological imperatives.

....

EXISTENTIAL LEVEL 2: *Tribal/Magical Thinking*

Theme: Sacrifice one's desires to the way of one's elders and ancestors.

Core Values: Safety, Tradition

Life Goal: Please the spirits and ensure continuance of the tribe.

....

EXISTENTIAL LEVEL 3: *Heroic Thinking*

Life Theme: Express one's self, to hell with consequences, lest one suffer the torment of shame.

Core Values: Power, Strength

Life Goal: Escape the suffocating dictates of tradition and achieve personal power/glory.

....

EXISTENTIAL LEVEL 4: *Absolutistic Thinking*

Life Theme: Sacrifice self now to receive later reward.

Core Values: Discipline, Authority, Purpose

Life Goal: Find peace and meaning in this world by denying impulses and upholding morality.

....

EXISTENTIAL LEVEL 5: *Individualistic Thinking*

Life Theme: Express self for what self-desires, but in a calculated fashion so as to avoid bringing down the wrath of important others.

Core Values: Accomplishing, Power, Profit

Life Goal: Achieve success and affluence in this life by strategically manipulating desired outcomes.

EXISTENTIAL LEVEL 6: *Humanistic Thinking*

Life Theme: Sacrifice self now in order to gain acceptance now.

Core Values: Equality, Honesty, Relatedness

Life Goal: Find happiness in this life—in this moment—by relating deeply to other humans.

EXISTENTIAL LEVEL 7: *Systemic Thinking*

Life Theme: Express self for what self desires and others need, but never at the expense of others, and in a manner that all life on the planet can continue to exist.

Core Values: Integrity, Competence, Sustainability

Life Goal: Restore vitality and balance to a world torn asunder.

EXISTENTIAL LEVEL 8: *Holistic Thinking*

Life Theme: Sacrifice the idea that one will ever know what it is all about and adjust to this as the existential reality of existence.

Core Values: Experience, Humility, Reverence

Life Goal: Surrender to the spiritual dimension underlying all forms.

It appears that most humans have an innate hard-wired physiological capacity to experience the world in each of the eight ways outlined above. In practice, we find that the majority of audiences in the so-called 'civilized' world can be understood by looking at Level #4 (absolutistic/navy) through Level #7 (systemic/gold). Understanding these different ways of making sense of the world gives a person terrific insight for framing messages that a given audience will experience as personally relevant.

The final equation authenticity + personal relevance = inspiration

Once we understand both the universals (similarities) and the specifics (differences), we have everything we need to consistently inspire all audiences. Please see Figure 8 on page 165. You'll notice that we've taken the dimensional model and expanded it to show the swirling expansion of mental space that humans experience over time as life pulls them upward and onward. This is the spiral of transformational growth that people's minds undergo as they learn to reinterpret the relationship between material and spiritual realities. With each step, the mind becomes a clearer and more expansive conduit for the emergence of energies from the causal, or spiritual realm.

Focus softly on the shape of this spiral and you may notice that it mirrors the swirling patterns of countless natural forms—from eddies in a rushing river stream, to storm clouds, to random whirls on a broken tree stump, to the Milky Way and beyond. This similarity was not consciously planned, nor is it surprising. Over time, the dynamic ebb and flow of human psychological evolution is just another example of nature's intelligence working to bring about change, growth and complexity. Just as rain and sun conspire to bring life to a tree, powerful communication design works with the forces of nature to foster the unfolding and emergence of life within the human being.

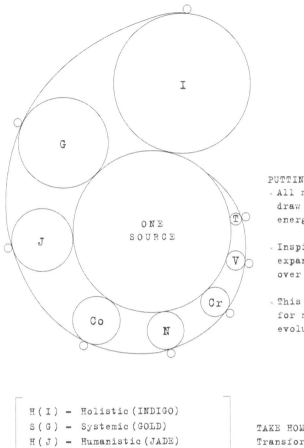

PUTTING IT ALL TOGETHER:
× All minds and bodies
  draw from one central
  energy bank (WHY)

× Inspiration leads to
  expanded cognitive space
  over time (HOW)

× This process accounts
  for mental and material
  evolution of mankind (WHAT)

H (I) — Holistic (INDIGO)
S (G) — Systemic (GOLD)
H (J) — Humanistic (JADE)
I (Co) — Individualistic (COPPER)
A (N) — Absolutistic (NAVY)
H (Cr) — Heroic (CRIMSON)
T (V) — Tribal (VIOLET)
A (T) — Autistic (TAN)

TAKE HOME MESSAGE:
Transformational Design
works with existing life
energies to be a catalyst
for inspiration, the emergence of life itself.

TRANSFORMATIONAL DESIGN SPIRAL
A BLUEPRINT FOR SOCIAL CHANGE
FIGURE: 8

CHAPTER 15

.....

Transformational Media in Five Steps

.....

"Inspiration exists, but it has to find you working."
- Pablo Picasso

In this chapter, we will spell out the specific steps that you'll follow to apply the Transformational Design framework to create inspiring new communications and solve real world challenges. Application of these principles always happens in one of three fundamental ways: organically, systematically, or (most commonly) through a mixture of both.

The *organic* path to creating inspired media is right-brain dominant and operates through spontaneous insight. As this framework sinks in, you start to generate penetrating vision into the hidden nature of people and things. As your intuition and authenticity improve, you will effortlessly learn to create and recreate inspiring new contexts for yourself and others without giving it a second thought. Inspiring others will become a cherished mental habit.

The *systematic* path to inspired media creation is left-brain dominant and operates through the specific application of a five-step design process that we will now outline. This process seamlessly integrates everything we've covered so far and lets us systematically bring our rational, analytical strengths to bear so that we can create a mental context that allows inspiration to strategically guide our creative (right-brain) efforts.

This chapter outlines the systematic approach. With practice and patience this thinking process will become intuitive, and the two paths will merge. The good news is that you'll always have this strong analytical system to fall back on should you ever get lost or mentally blocked.

Designing media from the inside out

If we view the path of experiencing inspirational communications as proceeding from the senses to the spirit, then we must conceive of the path for creating them as proceeding in exactly the opposite direction—from spirit, through the mind, to the senses. Why? Because spirit is the domain of intention, and in all creative endeavors intention is primary. It is the hidden force that drives the entire creative process. Taking this wisdom into account, the Transformational Design process starts with context and then builds outward according to the following five steps:

STEP 1: *Clarify Intentions*

First, we fully articulate our sponsoring vision. We must get clear about what we seek to create in all three dimensions (body, mind, and spirit), as well as our intentions for engaging the project.

STEP 2: *Define Target Audience*

Next, we use the Gravesian lens to better understand our target audience. How do they see the world? What are their values, tastes and preferences? What are their unique existential challenges?

STEP 3: *Create a Prototype*

Finally, we can throw our inner critic out the window and just let inspiration take the reins. We freely brainstorm the content of our message and put our ideas into working prototype form.

STEP 4: *Clean It Up*

Now we bring our left-brain back into the fray. We take our creative prototype, streamline, and polish it to make sure it is properly engineered to overcome all three filters.

STEP 5: *Test It Out*

Finally, we run our output up against an appropriate test audience to make sure it has the desired impact.

If followed with a spirit of authenticity and openness, you'll find that this simple process is a foolproof way of harnessing your deepest creative energies in the crafting of targeted, authentic, psychologically sophisticated communications. Steps 1 and 2 ensure that you properly define the creative context so that you will be personally inspired. Steps 3 and 4 help you direct that inspirational energy into the creation of streamlined media perfectly suited to your purpose. Step 5 helps you ensure that your final output has traction in the real world.

The metaphysical secret behind this approach is that the more time you spend on the hidden stuff (Steps 1 and 2), the more energy and vitality your end product will have. Why? Because clarifying intentions (Step 1) leads to authenticity and getting to know our audience (Step 2) enhances our ability to frame our message to generate a sense of personal relevance. Have I mentioned to you how important authenticity and personal relevance are for inspiration yet? Good. Just checking.

Now that you've gotten a grasp of the big picture, let's spend some time reviewing each step in greater detail.

....

Step 1: Clarify Intentions

They say that "The road to hell is paved with good intentions." For present purposes, this means that most campaigns are dead before they even leave the gate because they haven't originated from a clearly spelled-out creative vision that simultaneously resonates on every dimension. Our first task then is to use the three-dimensional model to spell out exactly what we want to create and why (our sponsoring motive).

Grab a blank piece of paper. Draw two lines across, cutting the paper into three large sections. At the top of the first section write: "What tangible outcomes do I want to create?" At the top of the second section write: "What attitudes and beliefs do I want to inspire?" At the top of the third section write: "What is my true motive for doing this?" (See the Appendix for example worksheets for this and all other steps.) Once you've got the template set up, you can start clearly defining your intentions by answering these three important questions, as outlined on the next page.

Inspiration in Action #31: The proof is in this pudding

Would you like to see a hands-on example of something that was created using the Transformational Design process? You're holding it! This book was created using the very same
process that it outlines. Does this mean that I just bullied through the five steps in a straight
line, from start to finish? Not quite. Due to job demands and sleep deprivation, I actually
tried to cut corners a few times. But each time—by some annoying law of creativity—inspiration would dry up. Whenever this happened, I would just revisit my original intentions again
and clear up some area of inauthenticity. Like magic, inspiration would reappear! This same
process can help a person resolve blockages in every life domain (relationships, professional, etc). The laws of creativity are as universal as the essence from which they arise.

Section 1: "What tangible outcomes do I want to create?"

In this section you will outline the material and behavioral outcomes
that your campaign is designed to create. Do you want to get people
to vote for your favorite political candidate? Do you want to sell a
boatload of environmentally safe widgets? Do you want to heal the
ennui of baby sea turtles? Whatever it is, write it down. Be as specific
and far ranging as possible. And, if your goals include making tons of
money, don't feel guilty. Write it down. There's nothing bad or good
here. We are simply defining the intended material outcomes. Be as
clear and thorough as possible. Precision counts.

Section 2: "What attitudes and beliefs do I want to inspire?"

Here you will outline your intended mental outcomes, as pertains to
your audience. How do you want them to feel about your idea, company, product, or service? Visualize the specific attitudes that you'd
love others to have and write them down. For example, let's say your
goal is to get people to buy a book that you are planning to write. How
do you want this book to show up for other people? What meaning
would it have for their lives? Will they be eager to tell their friends
about it? Will it lead them to a renewed interest in the subject matter?
Take some time to describe exactly what attitudes you wish to create.

Section 3: "What is my true motive for doing this?"
In this section you will honestly explore your reasons for choosing to initiate this particular creative endeavor. Quiet your mind. Look inside. Place your attention on the idea of the project. How does it make you feel? What about it excites you the most? What is it about the project that makes you feel uneasy? Write it all down free-form without editing or criticizing yourself. Be bold, be honest, be thorough—remember that no one else will ever need to see this.

Believe it or not, once you've fully answered these questions you will have come a long way on unseen levels. Writing about our intentions, if done honestly, can stir up emotions—ugly emotions. We see how secretly invested we are in manipulating others for personal gain, we see how real the idea of 'scarcity' is to us, we see how cynical we've become about truly making a difference. If any of this occurs to you while you're writing the final section—great! This means you're extracting the very poison that would have otherwise operated to secretly castrate your creative potency.

The fact is, writing about our intentions requires that we ask our minds to look inwards towards the spiritual dimension, which requires that we encounter the spiritual filter and all the guilt that surrounds it. We must distinguish and release this guilt to reach authenticity. The good news is that no matter what unpleasant emotions may surface, *your true hidden intention is always to serve others and to contribute.* You may not believe this, but it's true. You don't need to believe it. You just need to be *willing* to consider that it may be true and let your conscience do the rest.

The best way to accomplish this is to dig through the inner muck to discover the intention to serve that attracted you to this particular project in the first place. If you can't find that spirit of gratitude and service right away, keep at it. If you still can't find it, please consider that you are either 1) unwilling to find it, or 2) engaged in the wrong course of action. Make a choice to continue or discontinue the project accordingly. Nothing is more vital to the success of your creative endeavors than taking the time to get through to the core of inspiration that sparks you.

Before moving on to Step 2...

You'll want to clean up and clarify your intentions. Get out another clean sheet of paper. Write down the same three questions as before. Look over your first worksheet. What words and ideas resonate most? Highlight them. Soften your focus. Put the pieces together. Simplify and edit. Spend some time getting your intentions articulated in clean, clear sentences that inspire you. Read these sentences aloud. Make sure that you feel satisfied and inspired. You will probably use this sheet several more times before the creative process is complete.

....

Step 2: Define Target Audience

Once we've got intention lined up properly, we can take our attention off of ourselves and put it onto our audience. Using a combination of Graves' model and common sense, we will create a profile for our target audience that gives us a firm grasp of the values, aesthetics and metaphors that matter to them most. But our first task will be to clean out the cobwebs of our preexisting mental biases.

STEP 2A: *Clearing the slate*

Pull out another sheet of paper. Break it up into three sections, just like before. At the top of each section write down one of the following questions: "What kind of person would be most naturally interested in this message? Why?", "What kind of person would be most bored or ambivalent towards this message? Why?", "What kind of person would be the most hostile towards this message? Why?" Take a few minutes to answers these questions, free form, with little or no self-monitoring. (See Appendix for sample worksheets for this and all other exercises.)

Section 1: "What kind of person will be most naturally interested in this message? Why?"

Imagine someone just like you who shares your passion for this message (product, service, etc.) Why does it matter to them so much? What must've happened to make them see it this way? Write it all down. As you do this, make sure to focus as much as possible on the intangibles such as beliefs and attitudes and less on specifics such as age and demographics. To make it easier, you might want to imagine a specific person or character (real or fictional).

Section 2: "What kind of person will be most naturally bored or ambivalent towards this message? Why?"

When writing this section, imagine a person who is completely bored by and listless to your agenda. Every inspired thought, every passionate plea, every cherished value falls upon deaf ears. Note: this person isn't hostile, they are just unmoved. If you want to make things even more interesting, focus on someone with mixed feelings. He or she is drawn to your message on one level, but repelled by it on another. Perhaps you can think of a specific person or draw from someone in your life. Be curious. Take their perspective. Experience it.

Section 3: "What kind of person will be most hostile towards this message? Why?"

This step can be fun. Imagine someone who is actually offended by your message. Not bored, not ambivalent—but hostile. They have an irrational distaste for it. Why does your message cause such an unpleasant experience for them? What values and beliefs must they hold that would cause them to look at the world this way in relation to your message? Write it all down.

Assessing the social landscape

Once you've outlined audiences on every end of the spectrum, you are ready to step back and observe the complexity of the social landscape that confronts you. The most interesting thing about this process is that it has more to do with *you* than with your intended audience. By projecting your beliefs onto these hypothetical targets, you will see the hidden prejudices that you carry. You will see the contours of the current social map you hold in your mind. Not only will this help you clear the slate, but it will also help you develop a full, three-dimensional perspective on your message and give you a leg up on framing it for targeted audiences.

Compare and Contrast

The final task here is to review your answers to each question, focusing in on the specific values, attitudes and beliefs for each character profile. Highlight key words that stand out most in describing the mindset of the hypothetical audiences you have depicted. Once you've done this, it's time to match these three hypothetical character profiles up against the levels of existence defined in Part II. Briefly review the character sketches outlined in Chapter 10. Which existential levels/thinking systems match up best? Write your answers down in each section.

[*Quick note*: If your message is in any way progressive or life-affirming, you may find that your naturally receptive audience falls somewhere around the systemic/gold and the humanistic/jade existential levels. You may also find that your naturally ambivalent/bored and hostile audiences see the world through a mixture of individualistic/copper or absolutistic/navy lenses. Every situation is unique, but don't be surprised if, over time, this sort of pattern emerges.]

STEP 2B: *Target audience profiling*

Now that you've determined your audience's value landscape, you want to choose a target audience and prepare yourself to communicate with them. It may be helpful at this point to review the designated chapter in Part II that outlines the psychology and design strategies for your chosen target audience (Chapters 9-12). You'll now want to create a list of tactics and preferences that relate to this particular audience type. On a clean sheet of paper, answer the questions on the following page:

- *What are this target audience's core values and theme for living?*

- *What values most offend this audience? Why?*

- *What is this audience's preferred bottom line (purpose, profit, people or planet)? How might I use this? What's the next higher bottom line?*

- *How might situation and value-framing be used to create rapport with this audience?*

- *Based upon the research, what metaphors will resonate most with my audience's current worldview? What are some strengths and limitations of these metaphors?*

- *Based on the research, what is the transformational metaphor that might pull this audience up to a higher existential level?*

- *What type of "calls" resonate most with this thinking type (calls to duty, action or imagine)? How and where might these be applied?*

- *Are there any specific social or demographic variables (age, sex, income, education, profession, etc.) that should be considered? Why?*

Take the time to do this legwork. Use Part II of this book as a reference. When you are finished, you will have a terrific grasp of exactly who you are speaking to and how they think. You will also have created a customized audience map to guide you if you get blocked during the free-for-all creative process that follows.

Before moving on to Step 3...
Now you'll want to step back and clear your mind completely. You may even want to get a good night sleep or do whatever it takes to release this project for a little while. Because most creative work actually occurs in the subconscious, the information from Step 2 must percolate at a much deeper level than immediate awareness. Audience profiles and intention sheets such as the one you have now created are

most effective when we let them sink in and allow them to inform our creativity in a subtle, intuitive way. When we trust it, the subconscious is our most talented inner artist.

....

Step 3: Create a Prototype

In Steps 1 and 2, you created a thorough mental context for crafting a message that is both authentic and relevant to your target audience. Now you must be willing to let inspiration guide you. This requires that you turn inward and simply listen.

Grab a pen and paper, sit quietly and observe. Write down everything that comes to mind. Don't worry about being coherent, eloquent, clever, or polished. Turn off your inner critic and capture every crazy idea. Let the stream of unconscious images and sounds flood your mind and capture as many of them as you can. (Some might prefer to use a voice recorder or some other media to capture their thoughts, which is fine.)

If you want to introduce a little more structure to this process or if you don't have a clear direction yet, you can break your sheet up into a few sections with the following headings: "Images," "Sounds," "Words" and "Key Concepts." After each section, just write down whatever pops into your mind, trusting that all of it fits with some larger—yet unseen—pattern.

The important thing here is that you stop critical thinking and trust your fuzzy inner genius to deliver exactly the right information. If you stick with this, you'll eventually find a powerful—and perhaps unexpected—creative direction taking shape through you. Like one of Rorschach's inkblots, your ideas will holistically merge into a creative gestalt. On the surface, ideas may seem random and disconnected. But nothing is random. All ideas are caused by the force of creative intention. Having clearly defined your (material, mental and spiritual) intentions, now you must be willing to trust the results that they deliver.

The hidden secret of creativity is this: creative people are always excellent inner listeners. They have developed a habit of paying attention to their own inner creative impulses, and capturing them in representative forms (such as novels, pictures, movies, etc). The reason most people lose their creativity as they grow up is that they learn to tune out and stop trusting in the mind-frequency of their inner Leonardo da Vinci.

Before moving on to Step 4...

Step 3 isn't complete until you've developed and fleshed out one or more of your ideas. At this stage, your own inspiration is the litmus test for an idea's value. Of the information you've written, what stands out for you the most? Which direction seems as though it is the most emotionally powerful course to take? Which approach strikes you as being the most relevant for the mindset you seek to inspire?

Once you've found an inspired direction, spend some time elaborating it into a working prototype. Don't worry about getting things perfect. Just keep listening. Keep developing the idea through whatever means. If you get stuck, refer back to the intention worksheet (Step 1) and the audience profile (Step 2). These two documents are indispensable, because they will help reset the creative context and invite new inspiration, when needed. If reviewing these ideas doesn't immediately give you new insights, just rest your mind for a minute—take a walk, do the dishes, exercise or whatever—and a new idea will soon come up. Tend to your thoughts like a gardener tends to his or her garden, with patience and faith in nature's creative power.

[*Quick note*: As excited as you may be, please don't share your creative output with anyone else until after Step 4 is complete. Doing so pulls you out of the playful creative mode and will likely undermine your authenticity.]

Step 4: Clean It Up

If we liken Step 3 to the birthing process, Step 4 would be the part where we clear away the afterbirth. At this point we have created an authentic, inspired prototype designed specifically for a well-defined target audience. But we can't send it out into the world until we tweak and make sure every design element successfully serves our sponsoring vision. The dimensional model is a great tool for accomplishing this.

Please see Figure 9 on the opposite page. As you may recall from Chapter 3, this model conceptually spells out each step that our message must take before it can reach inspirational pay dirt. In Step 4, our task is to now use this schematic as a reference point for analyzing the strengths and weaknesses of our current message design. This requires that we perform assessments of two basic types: structural and experiential.

STEP 4A: *Performing Experiential Assessment*

To experientially assess our creative output's effectiveness, we should clear our mind and imagine that we are a member of our target audience [to get in character, you can review the audience checklist worksheet that you completed in step 2b]. From this perspective, we should encounter our output and ask ourselves the following three questions:

Question #1: "Does this message capture my attention?"

This question deals with overcoming the sensory filter. Your answer to this question is only going to be as good as your insight into your audience's aesthetic sensibilities and goals. Such intuitive perspective-taking ability will improve dramatically with practice.

Question #2: "Does this message seem urgent/personally relevant?"

This question deals with overcoming the mental filter. Given the target audience's values and the specific context in which the message will be experienced, would this message elicit a strong sense of urgency and relevance to personal goals? If you were a member of this audience, would it get you thinking and mentally engaged? Would you sense an opportunity to gain (or to avoid losing) something important?

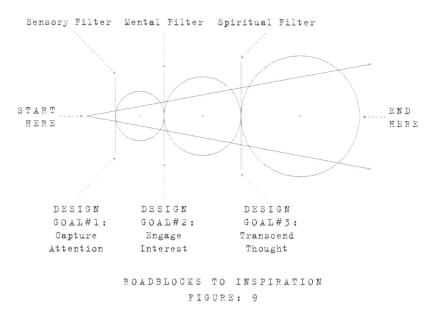

ROADBLOCKS TO INSPIRATION
FIGURE: 9

Question #3: "Does this message inspire me?"
This question deals with overcoming the spiritual filter. As an imagined audience member, does this message make you feel something deeply? Does it seem authentic? Does it move you to release your mental resistance and call you to embrace new life possibilities?

The holistic feedback you get from experiencing your own message from a new, imagined viewpoint will help you discover areas where your message may have missed the mark. Your answers to these three questions will set the groundwork for your left-brain to diagnose the concrete structural deficiencies and opportunities, as outlined in the following section.

***

STEP 4A: *Performing Structural Assessment*
Once you've gotten a global sense of your message's strengths and short-comings, it's time to get analytical. Like a scientist, you will objectively assess the structural quality of your message by asking a series of questions to evaluate specific design qualities and characteristics. These questions

provide a comprehensive set of checklists that take into account every available filter-opening tool according to the path laid out by Figure 9.

Question #1: "Does the message contain design elements that will overcome the sensory filter in your target audience?"

Examine your creative output to make sure you've taken advantage of every opportunity to include design qualities and motifs that will capture the attention and resonate with the aesthetic preferences of your audience. To make this easy, bounce your prototype up against the sensory filter checklist (Appendix, Worksheet 6a).

Question #2: "Does the message effectively use persuasive tactics that will overcome our target audience's mental filter?"

Now examine your creative output to make sure you've taken advantage of every opportunity to include framing and persuasive elements that resonate with the values and mindset of your particular target audience. When performing this assessment, bounce your prototype up against the mental filter checklist (Appendix, Worksheet 6b).

Question #3: "Does the output take advantage of tactics and strategies that will overcome the spiritual filter in our audience?"

Examine your creative output to make sure it effectively calls for your target audience to release their old perceptual context and adopt a new one. When performing this assessment, bounce your prototype up against the spiritual filter checklist (Appendix, Worksheet 6c)

The feedback you get from this analysis will help your left brain diagnose specific structural and tactical shortcomings of your message. This information will now be used to retool your message so that it seamlessly engages and overcomes all three filters.

Before moving on to Step 5...

As a result of these analyses, new ideas will surface. You will find that you've missed several opportunities to use powerful visual and rhetorical tools, and also included extraneous information that doesn't serve your purpose. Take the time to incorporate this corrective feedback into your message prototype. Add, subtract, edit, and refine your creative output until it tastefully reflects your new ideas and insights. Repeat this process until you've created a message that works. After each new iteration, take your message through the experiential analysis to make sure it effectively performs at each filter.

[*Quick note*: If at any point you get blocked, simply clear your mind, review your intention sheet (Step 1) and audience profile (Step 2), and then proceed again from Step 3. The best thing about this approach is that once you define your intentions and your audience, you've fashioned a sturdy creative context, or engine, that you can revisit again and again to ignite new inspiration as needed.]

Step 5: Test it Out

The final step is to take your creative output out into the real world to make sure it actually works. Getting test feedback can be a life-saving source of information, especially if you are designing media and messaging platforms for expensive, far-reaching campaigns.

From formal focus groups to informal peer reviews, there are countless ways to accomplish this final step. We will not spend much time discussing them here. Instead we will outline the general principles to consider when testing media from a Transformational Design perspective.

Principle #1: Consider the values of your audience.

Please keep in mind that your message is not generic. It has been customized for an audience with a particular worldview. The best test audience will be similar in values and worldview to the target audience that you are seeking to inspire. If you choose the wrong audience, your feedback will range from slightly inaccurate to awful.

For example, if you are designing an environmental campaign

that is seeking to make Democratic converts out of (navy-thinking) working class Republicans, don't expect to get accurate feedback by testing this commercial out with a group of (copper-thinking) white-collar executives. This audience is wired much differently. In fact, if you've done your job effectively, you should more likely expect to get a decidedly negative response from the latter.

If you can't find a group that accurately reflects your target, just use whatever audience you have and reinterpret their feedback based upon anticipated perceptual distortions that this audience brings to bear. Make specific predictions about how they will receive the message and keep these predictions in mind as you interpret the collected data. (*Quick note*: The audience analysis worksheets from Step 2b can be easily modified and repurposed as a profiling questionnaire for prospective target audience members.)

Principle #2: Ask questions to determine performance on each filter.
Your overriding objective when guiding focus groups is to determine how well your message performs on each successive filter. Make certain to ask questions that hit at the message's performance on each of these levels, in accordance with our "roadmap to inspiration" (Figure 9, page 179). In fact, what you will essentially do is apply the experiential assessment questions from Step 4 to a wider audience. However you choose to do it, make sure that you ask questions in accordance with our universal engagement sequence (senses/mind/spirit).

Also, note that you will probably never need to discuss the idea of "filters" with your audience, nor the concept of developmental value systems. These ideas are important for you, the communicator, but not for your target audience (unless, by coincidence, your audience is a group of gold-thinking people who wish to become better communicators, in which case please feel free to give me a call and I'll introduce you to some of my readers).

Principle #3: When in doubt, trust your gut.

How many times have we heard of great discoveries and breakthroughs that were ridiculed by the so-called 'experts'? At the end of the day, there is usually an element of brazen audacity in all inspired communication. Often it is the very thing that experts take issue with about your message that serves as the defining 'hook' that makes it work.

The bottom line? While you are testing your ideas out in the real world, make sure to temper your humility with a dose of foolhardy, self-confidence. If there's some particular aspect of your message that you find deeply compelling and yet you keep getting negative feedback about it, go with your gut. Chances are that you're onto something.

Transformational Design 'Lite'

Often times, instead of starting from scratch, we are tasked with fixing an existing speech, messaging platform or media campaign. Or perhaps we must work with a larger creative group and do not have much personal control over the creative direction. Fortunately, because our design framework is based on universal creative principles, it is infinitely adaptable to almost any context. In such situations, we can easily modify the above five step process, while still keeping our core principles intact.

One simple way to diagnose and fix an existing campaign is by applying the following three-step process:

STEP 1: *Perform target audience analysis*
Determine existing value systems operating in the target audience. What bottom lines are most relevant? What metaphors are most resonant? What situational factors will be most salient? (See Step 2 for a thorough review.)

STEP 2: *Perform Structural and Experiential Assessments*
Use target audience profile to structurally refine the message for its ability to overcome each successive filter. Use assessment feedback to

make structural changes and revisions to the campaign. (See Step 4 for a thorough review.)

STEP 3: *Test it out*

Did the changes work? Find an appropriately composed target group and get feedback as to the message's performance on each filter. Use feedback to edit message for optimal performance.

The great thing about this stripped down approach is that it can be universally applied, with relatively little effort, to any initiative whatsoever. The downside is that it is less thorough. Because it does not force us to take into account our sponsoring intentions (Step 1), we run a strong risk of operating from an inauthentic starting point. Feedback from this abbreviated process will be largely cosmetic and tactical. Such feedback may improve our message's effectiveness with target groups, but will be insufficient to ignite inspirational potency. The importance of authenticity cannot be overstated, as the root cause of inspiration is the gut realization that humans never truly need be inauthentic.

Inspiration in Action #32: Practice makes perfect

The term 'authenticity' looks great on paper, but being consistently authentic can be terribly difficult. (Especially if you're being authentic about it.) The mind can be a relentless little bugger in its quest to keep us enslaved to the material world. Here's the tough question: How can we possibly access the deepest layers of our audience's mind if we can't tap into the deepest layers of our own?...We can't. To consistently inspire, we must increase our capacity for authenticity by cultivating a daily habit of directly experiencing the spiritual plane. Which practice should you choose? I haven't the slightest idea. But in the 'Further Research' portion of the book you'll find a section entitled 'Mythology and Experiential Mysticism'. Here you'll find a list of resources that have worked well for me so far. Enjoy!

CHAPTER 16

.....

THE FUTURE OF INSPIRATION

.....

"All I know is that I don't know anything." - Socrates

All methods are traps. This book is no different. Yes, we've outlined the principles that underlie inspiration and have laid out a clear path for following them. And this path works. But, in the end, we must finally admit that the experience of inspiration and the power to ignite this feeling in others will always remain somewhat mysterious. Sometimes the best we can do is point our own minds towards the mystery and invite others to do so with us. But a good mystery is nothing to sneeze at! In the willing, mystery breeds a sense of wonder and humility, two sublime states mixing into a potent stew that lifts us towards an experiential realm that defies worldly thought.

What does this mean for those of us who must still lace up our Florsheims and shuffle to work each morning, rain or shine? It means that—mystery and all—we must make a firm commitment to never forget where our true power, our true leverage lies. True power lies forever beyond surface forms and circumstances, forever behind our shallow categories of thought. If we feel stifled by the economic and social conditions that seem to keep us trapped, let us pause to consider just how much transformative power we wield to change these conditions once we learn to view life from an inspirational lens.

The climate crisis, terrorism, racism, sickness, and drought—these are not problems, these are symptoms. The cause is hidden. We've designed it that way with a devious cleverness usually reserved for storybook villains. The true cause of our suffering is buried in our faulty notions about what it means to be human and our unwillingness to admit the truth of who we are. Inspiration is our remembrance of that simple, joyful truth.

Sound familiar? This was one of the first ideas that we covered in book's preface. In fact, it was the core insight that inspired the book itself, and mind-stopping theme branded upon every single page thereafter. To some people this lofty notion might seem grandiose or naive. But this book wasn't written for some people...it was written for you.

Correct me if I'm wrong, but you believe that communication should serve life, and not the other way around. You value authenticity and sustainability and you are tired of the hollow hype of traditional marketing tactics. You cringe at the notion that you must sacrifice your conscience in order to make a living. Ultimately, you care so deeply about the world we live in that you're willing to reexamine everything you think you know in order to help make it work. How do I know this? Because otherwise you wouldn't have read this book.

Marketing: It's not just for breakfast (foods) anymore

There was a time when marketing and communication skills were just handy tools helpful in pumping up profit margins. That time is gone. As a species, we now face unprecedented challenges to our very survival. Unbridled consumerism is eating up our planet, rabid religion is bringing out the worst bile in the human soul, and well-meaning idealists are too often enslaving the needy and empowering the vicious with their naive egalitarian agendas. But, beneath this bedlam, it still rings true that we are all merely humans seeking simple happiness and fulfillment.

So where's the disconnect?

The disconnect is in our minds, born of fear. Most of us are so caught up in fearful ideologies that we've lost the capacity to listen and be present to that deeper voice that knows the way. This disconnect has little to do with the world, and everything to do with us, with our ability to listen and experience the unchanging truth behind all forms. But here's the good news: truth is upon us. This book is one crest on an immense wave of truth that is crashing around our country and around the world, a tide of longing, a laugh in the face of bitterness, and a brazen stake to the claim of happiness that each of us carries innate.

Good ideas are wonderful, we need them. But the problem isn't our lack of good ideas, it's that we lack the motivation to follow through on the good ideas we already have. Inspired communication is our infinitely renewable fuel for implementing the good ideas that we must now collectively embrace if we wish for the human experiment to evolve upward to its next phase. Transformational Design is a new creative problem solving framework that will finally help us use media and communications to unleash this fuel for the betterment of all. I'm honored to be part of giving a voice to this inspired new paradigm, but must confess that I believe it to be just a humble beginning of something much larger.

So is there a moral to the story?

As I sit here trying to come up with a really poignant way to finish this book, my mind keeps getting distracted by an image that I haven't thought of in years—a toy. When I was eight, I was fixated on a particularly pointless toy. It was a small plastic football field scattered with a bunch of tiny plastic football players. When I'd press a button, the floor would start vibrating and all of the players would start moving around in jittery random patterns. On the surface it was a pretty boring toy, because the players just bounced around aimlessly. But still, I was transfixed.

This toy raised all manner of existential questions in my eight-year old brain: If the players didn't know where the goal was, how would the game ever end? How long was I supposed to sit there watching it? How would we ever find a clear winner? I was staggered by the implications. There I was, like a god—with just the click of a button—able to ignite the very life-force that animated these aimless hoards of polymer athletes...ON-OFF...ON-OFF..ON-OFF...Beyond the toddler power trip, I was smitten with the idea that each player was energized by the same underlying current. Did they ever stop to consider this? Probably not. What would happen if they did? If I relaxed my focus a bit, I could eventually observe ornate patterns emerging from the chaos. Were these players actually dancing? Was dancing somehow the hidden purpose of the game?!

If it sounds odd to you that an eight-year-old child would have such grandiose thoughts, then you've surely forgotten what it was like to be eight.

Kids are preternatural existentialists, perennially inspired by the universal implications of such ordinary realities as animated plastic toys and the hidden patterns of cereal bits as they float across milky cereal bowls.

Of course, sooner or later most children turn thirty. Instead of playing with tiny football toys, they go to live NFL football games. Instead of playing with cereal, they sit in meetings dreaming up new ways to sell cereal to children. As we get older, the games get bigger and scarier, but—as with the players in the plastic football field—our animating force stays constant. It can be both sad and funny to see that most of us are a lot like those plastic toy players: seeking an uncertain goal post on one large vibrating field, spinning in circles, holding our little footballs, wondering where all of the energy comes from and where—at the end of the day—it all goes.

But here's the real question for weary adults who still hope to reach the end zone: In the end, are we the plastic football player, or are we the curious eight year old with his finger on the button? Or are we, perhaps, both?

I don't know. I'm asking.

A brief flicker of terrifying bliss

September 10th, 2001. Almost a quarter century after I left the plastic toy behind, I found myself unemployed and living in New York City. I'll admit it—I was lost. My inner eight year old was grounded. The economy was collapsing and my unemployment checks were not enough to cover the student loan payments coming due. What was a somewhat privileged, unemployed, red-blooded, overly educated, late twenties philosophical escape artist to do? I rambled down to the corner pub and threw back many pints. Then I stumbled home and went to bed.

That night I had a dream. In this dream massive buildings collapsed. Bodies were mangled. Endless corpses were tangled in a dense thicket of steel, fire and smoke. Then, all of sudden, the earth from space. A hole opened up in the side of our planet and a steady stream of robed adults in graduation caps climbed out. They walked up to a lectern and accepted diplomas, each of them. I felt deeply proud of them, because—in dying— they had somehow accomplished exactly what they came here to do. They were now invisible to the rest of us, but still very much alive. It was a heartbreaking, bittersweet dream. I woke up crying. I didn't know why.

I wrote the dream down. I sketched a picture of the planet, the graduation caps, etc., and then set out to grab breakfast at a local diner. Halfway through my omelet, I heard the diner's cheap clock radio report that a small commuter plane had accidentally crashed into the World Trade Center's north tower. I looked out the diner window and there it was, sure enough...a gaping black cavity fuming at the top one of that shimmering corporate sky-tooth. How could I have known that I was about to undergo an experience that would change me—and the world— forever?

Don't worry. I'm not going to recant the whole drama with cliche's and morbid longings. But I will tell you this—words will never quite capture the mind-melting experience that I underwent living in New York City on that surreal day. It was as if I'd spent my entire life hypnotized and had finally been jolted awake to witness the joyful truth behind the mesmerizing curtain of fear and form...as if we, all of us, had been rushing headlong down a murky river stream, and suddenly grabbed at a branch above the water and pulled ourselves upward for a first-ever full breath of clear sunlit air. I know this might sound odd, considering all of the horror that went down, but that's exactly what it felt like. In the center of all that ugly—complete and utter freedom. Perhaps you felt it too?

I don't know. I'm asking.

How long will it take before we recapture that truth we so quickly buried under bricks of hostility and resignation? How many more disasters will it take before we finally wake up and pay homage to what's real? How many people thinking in concert will it take to forgive the fear and hatred that lingers still in our collective shadow? How great will it be when we finally stop pretending like there's anything going on in this world that we didn't—at some level—ask for and gracefully receive?

We are all so damn lucky to be alive.

When will we get off our high horse and finally admit that?

For those with the gumption to look, September 11th, 2001 was a beautiful beginning. It was a flickering-but-profound foreshadowing of our future life together: a life of truth over fear, a life without boundaries and stupidity and silly divisions that distract us from what's real, life as an expression of gratitude towards the source that inspires us all, effortlessly, from cradle to grave, without asking for a damn thing in return.

I'll admit, though…

I do worry.

Like you, I worry about the environment, the economy, terrorism, and all of that stuff. But more often I wonder—I wonder how it is possible that we could all be so deeply connected behind the thin veil of separation without experiencing it on a daily basis, and I wonder when we will collectively manage to recapture that sense of unity once again. The promise is certain, but the path is ours to make, and to remake until we get it right. I can't predict the future, but I can tell you this: the quickest and most joyful path will always be inspiration.

If we let it, inspiration will be the thread that leads us all gently out of the maze of confusion that we created when we first started pretending to be anything other than eight-year-olds finding meaning in nothing and infinity in the mundane. I'm sure that when enough of us finally choose to grab this thread and follow it back home again—to the truth—the flickering promise that we briefly felt beneath the chaos of September 11th will finally be fulfilled. I'm excited to meet you there.

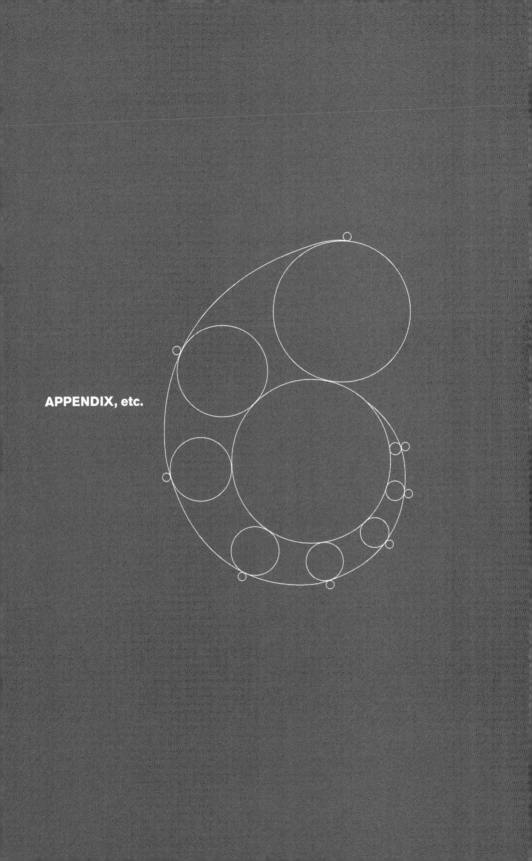

APPENDIX, etc.

APPENDIX

In the following pages you'll find worksheets templates and checklists to help you work through the creative exercises described in Chapter 15. These are as follows:

TEMPLATE 1 - *Intentions Worksheet*
(For use with Step 1)

TEMPLATE 2 - *Social Landscape Worksheet*
(For use with Step 2a)

TEMPLATE 3 - *Target Audience Checklist*
(For use with Step 2b)

TEMPLATE 4 - *Free Associations Worksheet*
(For use with Step 3 – if needed)

TEMPLATE 5 - *Experiential Assessment Worksheet*
(For use with Step 4a)

TEMPLATE 6 - *Structural Assessments Worksheets (3 templates)*
(For use with Step 4b)

Feel free to expand or alter these templates to suit your needs, just be sure to keep intact the three-dimensional structure implicit in the Transformational Design approach.

.....

TEMPLATE 1
Intentions Worksheet

.....

Defining your Vision

(please answer questions below in the space provided)

What specific material outcomes do I want to create?

What attitudes and beliefs do I want to inspire?

What is my true motive for doing this?

. . . . .

Template 2
Social Landscape Worksheet

. . . . .

Assessing the Social Landscape

(please answer questions below in the space provided)

What kind of person will be most naturally interested in this message? Why?

What kind of person will be most naturally bored by this message? Why?

What kind of person will be most naturally hostile towards this message? Why?

. . . . .

TEMPLATE 3
Target Audience Checklist

. . . . .

Profiling your Audience

(Using Graves research as a starting point, fully answer questions listed below on a separate sheet. Refer to chapters 9-12 for assistance.)

What are this target audience's core values and theme for living?

What values most offend this audience? Why?

What is this audience's preferred bottom line (purpose, profit, people or planet)? How might I use this? What's the next higher bottom line?

How might situation and value-framing be used to create rapport with this audience?

Based upon the research, what metaphors will resonate most with my audience's current worldview? What are some strengths and limitations of these metaphors?

Based on the research, what is the transformational metaphor that might pull this audience up to a higher existential level?

What type of "calls" resonate most with this thinking type (to duty, action, or imagine)? How and where might these be applied?

Are there any specific social or demographic variables (age, sex, income, education, profession, etc.) that should be considered? Why?

. . . . .

TEMPLATE 4

Free Associations Worksheet (optional)

. . . . .

(Clear your mind. Take a breath. Close your eyes. Listen and observe. Write whatever comes up.)

images

sounds

words

key concepts

. . . . .

TEMPLATE 5

Experiential Assessment Worksheet

. . . . .

Defining your Audience

(Please answer the following questions about your creative output from the perspective of a target audience member)

Does this message capture my attention? Why or why not?

Does this message seem urgent and personally relevant? Why or why not?

Does this message call upon me to experience something larger? Why or why not?

. . . . .

TEMPLATE 6A

Structural Assessment (Sensory Filter Checklist)

. . . . .

(Analyze your message according to the following questions in order to assess sensory filter design qualities.)

Sensory Filter:

Will your communication create an element of surprise?

Are your tone and style appropriate for your audience?

Have you created captivating sensory hooks?

Have you chosen an appropriately captivating media type for this message?

Have you created an appropriately captivating media placement strategy?

Notes:

.....

TEMPLATE 6B

Structural Assessment (Mental Filter Checklist)

.....

(Analyze your message according to the following questions in order to assess mental filter design qualities.)

Mental Filter Checklist

Does your message use situational framing to draw your target audience's attention into the moment and create mental rapport?

Does your message use questions to capture your target audience's interest?

Does your message use value framing to speak to the specific value and beliefs of your audience?

Does your message create a problem that will resonate with your target audience?

Does your message gracefully employ metaphors that will specifically resonate with your intended audience?

Does your message invoke the mesmerizing capacities of storytelling?

Notes:

.....

TEMPLATE 6C

Structural Assessment (Spiritual Filter Checklist)

.....

(Analyze your message according to the following questions in order to assess spiritual filter design qualities.)

Spiritual Filter Checklist

Does your message seem authentic and heartfelt?

Does your message employ humor to disarm the target audience?

Does your message deliver unspoken truths that might help build trust?

Does your message demonstrate that you trust the audience?

Does your message use repetition, rhyme, and other rhythmic elements that may have a hypnotic, mind-relaxing effect on the audience?

If your message raises a problem, does it offer real, inspiring solutions?

If your message tells a story, does that story have a powerful thematic climax?

Does your message ask the audience to look at limitations of old metaphors?

Does your message ask the audience to consider new transformational metaphors?

Does your message contain an effective call to action, duty, or imagine?

Does your message effectively use silence or empty space?

Notes:

Further Research

This book is an interdisciplinary synthesis of thinking from several different fields, including physiology, physics, psychology, systems theory, branding, business communication, mysticism and political science. The following pages list a small sampling of works that have shaped my thinking over the years. I've chosen them as a good starting point for those of you who might wish to do further exploration.

Clare W. Graves

Beck, Don and Christopher Cowan. *Spiral Dynamics: Mastering Leadership, Values, and Change.* Wiley-Blackwell, 2005.

Beck, Don. *Spiral Dynamics Integral: Learning How to Master the Memetic Codes of Human Behavior.* Audio 6 CD set produced by Sounds True Audio, 2006. (available at www.amazon.com)

Beck, Don. *Spiral Dynamics Integral: A Challenge to Leadership.* Video interview with Tom Feldman produced by Clearfire Media, 2006. (available at www.amazon.com)

Graves, Clare W. *The Never Ending Quest: Dr. Clare W. Graves Explores Human Nature* (with Christopher C. Cowan & Natasha Todorovic, Eds.) ECLET Publishing, 2005.

Graves, Clare W. *Levels of Human Existence.* ECLET Publishing, 2005.

(For more information on Graves, free articles, and product ordering info please visit www.clarewgraves.com and www.spiraldynamics.net.)

Business Communication and Branding

Hanlon, Patrick. *Primal Branding: Create Zealots for Your Brand, Your Company, and Your Future.* Patrick Hanlon. Free Press, 2006.

Lindstrom, Martin. *Brand Sense: Build Powerful Brands through Touch, Taste, Smell, Sight and Sound.* Free Press, 2005.

Neumeier, Robert. *The Brand Gap.* Peachpit Press, 2005.

Pine, Joseph B. and James H. Gilmore. *The Experience Economy: Work is Theater and Every Business is a Stage.* Harvard Business School, 1999.

Rackham, Niel. *SPIN Selling.* McGraw-Hill, 1988.

Soloman, Robert C. and Flores, Fernando. *Building Trust: In Business Partnership and Life.* Oxford University Press, 2003.

Science and Natural Systems

Bateson, Gregory. *Mind and Nature: A Necessary Unity.* Hampton, 2002.

Bertalanfy, Ludwig Von. *General Systems Theory: Foundations, Development, Applications.* George Braziller, 1976.

Bohm, David. *Wholeness and the Implicate order.* New York: Routeledge, 2002.

Bohm, David. *On Dialogue.* New York: Routeledge, 2004.

Kafatos, Menos and Robert Nadeau. *The Conscious Universe: The Part and the Whole in Modern Physical Theory.* Springer, 1999.

Capra, Frijtof. *The Web of Life: A New Scientific Understanding of Living Systems.* Anchor, 1997.

Chopra, Deepak. *Ageless Body, Timeless Mind: The Quantum Alternative to Growing Old.* Harmony, 1994.

Gleik, James. *Chaos: The Making of a New Science.* Penguin, 1988.

Talbot, Micheal. *The Holographic Universe.* Harper Perennial, 1992.

Varela, Francisco J. *The Embodied Mind.* MIT Press, 1991.

Psychology

Csikszentmihalyi, Mihaly. *Flow: The Psychology of Optimal Experience.* Harper Perennial, 1991

Csikszentmihalyi, Mihaly. *The Evolving Self: A Psychology for the Third Millennium.* Harper Perennial, 1994.

Hillman, James. *The Dream and the Underworld.* Harper Paperbacks, 1979.

Jung, Carl Gustav. *Archetypes and the Collective Unconscious* (R.F.C. Hull, translator). Princeton University Press, 1981.

Jung, Carl Gustav. *The Essential Jung* (Anthony Storr, editor). Princeton University Press, 1999.

Kegan, Robert. *The Evolving Self: Problem and Process in Human Development.* Harvard University Press, 1982.

Pervin, Lawrence A. *The Science of Personality.* Oxford University Press, 2002.

Messaging for Artists and Activists

Egri, Lajos. *The Art of Dramatic Writing.* Wildside Press, 2007.

Earle, Richard. *The Art of Cause Marketing: How to Use Advertising to Change Personal Behavior and Public Policy.* McGraw-Hill, 1992.

Lakoff, George. *Thinking Points: Communicating our American Values and Vision.* Farrar, Straus and Giroux, 2006.

Lakoff, George. *Don't Think of an Elephant: Know Your Values and Frame the Debate—The Essential Guide for Progressives.* Chelsea Green, 2004.

Luntz, Frank. *Words that Work: It's Not What You Say, it's What People Hear.* Hyperion, 2006.

McKee, Robert. *Story: Substance, Structure, Style, and the Principles of Screenwriting.* Harper Entertainment, 1997.

Shellenberger, Micheal and Ted Nordhaus. *Breakthrough: From the Death of Environmentalism to the Politics of Possibility.* Houghton Mifflin Co., 2007.

Westin, Drew A. *The Political Brain: The Role of Emotion in Deciding the Fate of the Nation.* Public Affairs, 2007.

Mythology and Experiential Mysticism

Anonymous. *A Course In Miracles.* Course in Miracles Society, 1972.

Campbell, Joseph. *The Inner Reaches of Outer Space: Metaphor as Myth and as Religion.* New World Library, 2002.

Campbell, Joseph and Bill Moyers. *The Power of Myth.* Anchor, 1991.

Chopra, Deepak. *Seven Spiritual Laws of Success: A Practical Guide to the Fulfillment of Your Dreams.* New World Library/Amber-Allen Publishing, 1994.

Hale, Dwoskin. *The Sedona Method.* Sedona Press, 2003.

Huxley, Aldous. *The Perennial Philosophy.* Harper Perennial, 2004

Sanchez, Nouk and Tomas Vieira. *Take Me to Truth: Undoing the Ego.* O Books, 2007.

Tolle, Eckhart. *The Power of Now: A Guide to Spiritual Enlightenment.* New World Library, 2004.

END NOTES

1. From the William Blake poem 'Auguries of Innocence'.

2. Two excellent books that discuss overcoming the sensory filter as it pertains to branding and corporate identity are *Brand Sense* by Martin Lindstrom and *Primal Branding* by Patrick Hanlon (see further research for info). Although these books also deal with deeper aspects of persuasion and inspiration, they primarily emphasize sensory data as the central leverage point for influencing the consumer psyche.

3. My thinking on this topic has been greatly influence by the book *SPIN Selling* by Niel Rackham (see further research for info). It's a dry read, but contains quite powerful, scientifically derived insights into the qualitative relationship between questions and persuasion.

4. My thinking on this topic has been greatly influenced by the writings of Lester Levenson. For a quick introduction to Lester Levenson's unique life and philosophy, read *No Attachments, No Aversions: The Autobiography of a Master* (see further research for info).

5. From *Macbeth* by William Shakespeare.

6. Quote taken from Graves Original research published in *The Never Ending Quest*, edited by Christopher Cowan and Natasha Todorovic (see further research for info).

7. These theme statements are the same, or slightly reworded versions of those directly outlined in *The Never Ending Quest*, edited by Christopher Cowan and Natasha Todorovic.

8. Estimates were extrapolated from Graves' research data as presented in *The Never Ending Quest*, edited by Christopher Cowan and Natasha Todorovic. Graves' figures were based upon systematic analysis of College Student populations from the late 1960's and early 70's.

9. Interestingly, Graves found that many serious drug and alcohol addictions occur in copper thinkers as they get lost in the transition from individualistic/copper to humanistic/jade thinking, as outlined in *The Never Ending Quest*, edited by Christopher Cowan and Natasha Todorovic (ECLET Publishing, 2005).

10. This multiple bottom-lines concept has been widely covered in many various professional books and articles. Most applications focus only on three: profits, people, and planet. These often fail to grasp the importance of a transcendent purpose for motivating sustainable human behavior..

INDEX

ABOUT THE AUTHOR

John Marshall Roberts teaches people and organizations how to overcome cynicism and inspire. He has a master's degree in organizational psychology and more than decade of strategic communications consulting experience. An avid musician, acclaimed speaker, and closet research geek, John is gripped with the idea that transformational communication holds the key to unleashing a new breed of global leadership from the grass roots level upward. He never tires of discussing this vision in front of audiences, giving workshops for socially and environmentally conscious leaders, or applying his unique research tools to the creation of results-driven campaigns. For more information about John, and the latest on Transformational Design® products and services, visit John's blog at www.jmarshallroberts.com.

Made in the USA
Lexington, KY
06 June 2011